TREASURE HUNTING

BY JOSHUA E. BISHOP

PO Box 83, Ormond Beach, FL 32175 :: rwipublishing.com

To my children:

Pursuing Christ as your father has become the greatest treasure I've ever found. I thank God for the privilege of loving you, leading you, and watching Him work in you.

CONTENTS

CHAPTER ONE

HIDDEN TREASURE

In 1622, a Spanish ship called the Nuestra Señora de Atocha sank off the coast of Florida, loaded with unimaginable riches: gold bars, silver coins, emeralds, and many other priceless artifacts. For centuries, that treasure lay buried under the sea, hidden and unreachable. Its story had since faded into legend.

Enter Mel Fisher. In 1969, Fisher and his crew began what seemed like a foolish dream—hunting for the Atocha's treasure. Month after month, year after year, they searched the ocean floor. The hunt stretched into decades. They endured storms, equipment failures, and even personal tragedy. People called him crazy. But Fisher had a motto: "Today's the day." Every morning, he would rally his team with those words. Not someday. Not maybe. Today.

On July 20, 1985, after sixteen years of digging, diving, and disappointment, the dream became reality. They uncovered what was dubbed the "Motherlode." Hundreds of millions of dollars' worth of treasure: gold chains, emerald-studded crosses, and over forty tons of silver. It was one of the greatest treasure finds in modern history.

I'll never forget standing, just a couple of years ago, inside the Gaylord Palms in Kissimmee, Florida. My family was on vacation, and they had some of Mel Fisher's treasure on display. Behind thick glass sat gleaming gold bars and brilliant emeralds—treasures that had been hidden beneath the crashing waves for centuries, until Fisher's team brought them to light.

I remember picking my daughter up so she could press her nose against the glass, her eyes wide as she stared at real treasure. Not pretend treasure. Not movie props. But the actual gold and jewels that had once been lost to the sea. In that moment, I felt wonder, as if I too were just a child pressing my nose against the glass. Not just because of the gold, but because of the joy of sharing that wonder with her, my son, and my wife. The kingdom—Christ Himself as the King—is that treasure, and nothing compares.

The hunt wasn't only about what Mel Fisher found, it was about how he found it. Daily resolve. Joyful anticipation. Sacrifice that looked foolish to everyone else. But that sacrifice made perfect sense once the treasure was uncovered.

The power of treasure is that it captures the heart. Unearthing it makes every sacrifice seem worth it. That's why Mel Fisher's story fits so perfectly because it sets up the greater story Jesus told: that the kingdom of heaven is like treasure hidden in a field.

A man stumbles across some sort of amazing treasure. He buries it again, and then, in his joy, sells all that he has and buys the field. To the outside world, it looked ridiculous. Who sells everything for a plot of dirt?

But that man knew the truth: the treasure beneath the surface outweighed everything else.

That's where our adventure begins.

Matthew 13:44
Jesus said, "The kingdom of heaven is like treasure hidden in a field, which a man found and covered up. Then in his joy he goes and sells all that he has and buys that field."

The word Jesus uses for "treasure" is the source of our word thesaurus, which means, for us, a treasury of words. It doesn't mean a handful of loose coins jingling in a pouch; it means riches of surpassing worth, a hoard of valuables so great it changes the life of whoever finds it. Jesus is making a staggering claim.

Notice that the treasure was "hidden in a field." It wasn't obvious, and it wasn't flashy. The world passed by that field day after day, never realizing what lay beneath the soil. That's how it is with Christ. His worth is veiled to many until God opens their eyes by grace. To most, He looks like a wandering rabbi or a good teacher. But to those whose eyes are opened, He is the Pearl of great price (Matt. 13:45– 46). He Himself is the Treasure beyond all treasures. The heartbeat of the parable is; the surpassing worth of Christ makes every sacrifice not just reasonable, but joyful.

My wife and I were newly married, and all of a sudden I found myself out of a job. I was fired just before Thanksgiving 2005, and we had a little savings which got us almost through the holidays. Finding a new job proved much harder than I would have wanted, so Sarah and I did odd jobs and handyman work to put food on the table. Had it not been for the kindness of our families, we would not have done as well as we did through those following six or seven months.

It was then I finally got hired by a start-up company. I would be working about thirty minutes away from my apartment at the VP's house, in his son's room that had been borrowed to start the company. I would find out that I was the company's first hired employee. I would be their first customer service agent. I could have been hired to scrub the floors and been happy about it. It wasn't but a few weeks into the job that Kyle walked into the room and thanked me for a job well done. He said he'd love to give me a raise, but there just wasn't any money for that now. He did make me a promise. "A rising tide raises all boats." I understood instantly and became even more grateful and excited to have hitched my wagon to Bridge2 Solutions.

A few months later I began steadily preaching at Calvary Baptist Church in Daytona Beach. Their pastor, Gary Goad, had developed cancer, and after his chemotherapy treatments, he was just too tired to prepare sermons, let alone preach. As I was on the local Baptist association's rotating fill-in list, I was asked to fill in once for him. One time became three, and then the deacons began to just call me to fill in when Gary was out.

Christmas 2007, Sarah and I were at Calvary for their Christmas service. We had enjoyed the people, and they seemed to enjoy our company as well. Gary was sitting on an elevated chair behind the pulpit and was preaching a wonderful message about the Savior we needed, who had finally come. Abruptly, maybe fifteen minutes into his message, he stopped. The world's longest ten seconds went by, and he said, "I need someone to come and get me. I can't go on." Gary would be helped down, the service was concluded, and he would have his wife call the deacons the next day to officially step down.

That same week, the deacons would call me and ask if I'd be willing to step in as the interim pastor while they looked for a new one. Without hesitation, I said yes. A couple of weeks went by, and the deacons came up to me and asked if I'd consider being their pastor even though they could only pay me $400 a month. My wife and I were thrilled to say yes.

It was January of 2009, and the church was growing. I had helped Kyle hire and train a full team of customer service agents that filled an office in a new part of town. We had grown so much that Kyle needed to promote me officially. Sarah and I had already begun saving money and planning on making a go at the church "full-time." I had spoken to the deacons and told them that if they could pay me $1,200 per month, coupled with Sarah's salary, that would cover my bills enough so that I could quit my other job and devote myself fully to ministry.

Kyle invited me into his office. He asked if I remembered the comment he'd made just about a year and a half ago. He said, "Josh, you've helped raise that tide, and I want to offer you…" I stopped him. I told him what Sarah and I had been praying about and that we were aiming at ministry. He then responded with what the tide would be, and it was a rather high sort of tide.

I've had times in the last eighteen years when I've thought back on that moment and wondered what my life would be like had I not so kindly but quickly shot Kyle down. February 5, 2020, the company was acquired by a Fortune 500 company, Intercontinental Exchange, for just under 300 million dollars. I couldn't have known that kind of valuation, nor could I assume I would have stayed or risen in the ranks enough to benefit from the sale, but that's the kind of tide I turned down.

When I left Bridge2 Solutions in April of 2009, it was not a sad goodbye. It was a celebration. There was even a cake. I encouraged the people around me to celebrate with Sarah and me because we were genuinely excited about what came next. To show just how excited we were, I had already booked and paid for a fifth-anniversary trip to the Ritz-Carlton in Amelia Island, just a month and a half after leaving B2S. But even that trip got cut short. We were so eager to get started that we left early and came home to get back to work at the church.

In Matthew 13, Jesus explains the man's motivation: "in his joy." This man doesn't sell everything because he's forced to. He doesn't walk away with a long face, muttering about what he's lost. Joy is the engine of his sacrifice. Joy makes the giving up seem small compared to the gaining. And this is exactly what separates true Christianity from lifeless religion. Duty trudges along because it has to, but joy sells all because it gets to.

"He sells all that he has." That's renunciation. He lets go of everything. He lets go of all his security, his possessions, even what he likely valued most—comfort. But not to earn the treasure. This isn't a works-based purchase; it's a value-based exchange. He sees what's in the field and gladly parts with everything else because, compared to Christ, nothing else compares.

Finally, "he buys that field." The cost is total. No half-measures. He doesn't haggle, doesn't offer a portion. He surrenders everything because he knows the exchange is infinitely worth it. That's the call of discipleship. Christ is not added onto an already full life; He becomes your life.

True Treasure

When Jesus tells us the kingdom is like treasure hidden in a field, he's not dangling streets of gold or a mansion in the sky in front of us. Those things are real, but they're not the reward. The treasure isn't a crown to wear, it's not a gate of pearl to walk through, and it's not even the joy of seeing loved ones again. The treasure is Christ Himself.

Charles H. Spurgeon said it well: "It is better to have our good God than all the goods in the world: it is better to have God for our all than to have all and be without Him." That's the point Jesus makes here. The man in the field isn't rejoicing because he found a better lifestyle, or a safer future. He's rejoicing because he found something so valuable that everything else could finally be seen for what it was. Lesser treasures are not evil in themselves, but they are lesser. They can't bear the weight of our souls. They can't forgive sin. They can't satisfy the heart. They can't raise the dead. But Christ can. Christ does. To have Him is to have the treasure beneath every other promise God has made.

Paul captures this so clearly in Philippians 3:7–8:

"But whatever gain I had, I counted as loss for the sake of Christ. Indeed, I count everything as loss because of the surpassing worth of knowing Christ Jesus my Lord."

We should hear the echo of the man in the parable. Paul isn't begrudging what he lost. He calls everything else loss because of the surpassing worth of Jesus. What gain do you have that hasn't first been given to you by Christ? What work have your hands accomplished that were not actually empowered by Christ's hands? Any wealth or accomplishments, and riches we could claim, haven't they actually been a gracious gift to begin with?

This is why Jesus says in Matthew 13, "in his joy he sold all." Following Jesus isn't grim resignation; it's a joyful pursuit. Duty without delight is a lifeless religion. But when your eyes have seen the treasure, joy compels you to act. The universal act of seeing Jesus as the treasure He really is? Renunciation. Renouncing our goals for His goals. Renouncing our purpose for the one He has laid upon us. Even renouncing the joys of eternity, for the sake of Christ Himself.

Consider that even the most dazzling ideas of what heaven might look like pale in comparison to the person of Jesus. Have you not noticed that the streets of gold are such because gold is regarded as just pavement. Massive pearls are nothing but chain-link fencing. Shiny rewards are great, but they aren't ultimate. Jesus is ultimate. The Christian life isn't about collecting heavenly trinkets, but about gaining Christ—more of him and less of us.

When you treasure Christ above all, everything else falls into its rightful place. Loss becomes gain, sacrifice becomes joy, and suffering becomes the seeds of glory. What you treasure here changes the way you measure everything. In one of C. S. Lewis' most prolific books, Mere Christianity, he put it this way; "Look for Christ, and you will find Him, and with Him everything else thrown in."

This is what it means to be a real treasure-hunter. It means to see Christ as worth more than every earthly possession, every passing pleasure, and every fleeting glory. He is the reward. He is the treasure.

Hold Loosely
If, and when I say if I mean since, Christ is the treasure, then the first question every believer must ask is, "What other things am I clinging to instead of Him?" The man in the parable didn't hesitate. He didn't hedge his bets. He sold all because he knew the treasure outweighed everything else. What about us?

Let's be honest. False treasures are scattered everywhere, and our hearts are so quick to chase them. Some are ancient and timeless, like the desire for comfort, the lust for control, the hunger for money, the applause of man, and the pull of relationships. Others are distinctly modern, such as the endless scrolling that numbs our attention, the dream of career success that quietly becomes our identity, the idol of leisure and convenience, or the craving for online approval measured in likes and followers. None of these things last, yet how often do we hold them as if they were life itself?

I have a few questions I want you to answer. Find a scrap of paper and something to write with. No, I mean it. You should literally stop reading for a second, find a pencil, grab a scrap of paper, and actually write the answers down. Just reading the questions and thinking about them in your head will not have the same effect. I can't tell you how many times I've read books like this, hit a section with questions, and just politely skipped right over them like the author wasn't talking to me. Don't do that.

Also, don't write the answers in the book. If you do, you might be tempted to soften the truth a little in case you lend this copy to someone later. Use a scrap of paper. Be honest there. Nobody has to see it but you and the Lord.
Don't worry. I'll wait right here.

Now that you have something to write with and something to write on, here are the questions.

- What do you lose that makes you panic?
- What do you guard that you can't imagine surrendering?
- What do you daydream about when your mind drifts?

Those questions expose what you treasure.

I'll answer these questions for myself, at the time of me writing here.

What do you lose that makes you panic?
Context. Or I could say understanding. It seems ridiculous, but when I'm out of the loop on things, I find myself panicking to understand what's going on. I think that might have its basis in control, which is to say pride. I guess if I know what's going on all the time around me, I'll be able to fix or direct things the way I want them to go.

What do you guard that you can't imagine surrendering?
My family. It's an easy answer, I know, but it was the knee-jerk response I'm looking for out of you, the reader. As my kids get older, it's harder and harder to imagine them leaving the nest. I want to protect them from the world and pain. I want to keep their eyes from the evil my eyes have seen and their hearts from the pain I've felt. That's not wrong in itself. Family is a gift from the Lord. But even good gifts can become something we clutch as if they are ours to keep absolutely.

What do you daydream about when your mind drifts?
Bridge2 Solutions. Just kidding. I mean, not really, when you boil it down. I guess, like many men, I dream of success. I daydream of accolades and praise. I daydream of contributing something significant to the world before I leave it. I want to make a lasting mark so that when I'm dead, people might think of me and what I've done with fondness. But then I'm reminded of what Nikolaus Ludwig von Zinzendorf und Pottendorf taught: "Preach the gospel, die, and be forgotten."

When we live as true treasure hunters, we begin to see Jesus as better. Better than control. Better than comfort. Better than success. Better even than the good gifts we're tempted to clutch with both hands. And if Jesus is better, then life has to be reordered around Him. Our schedules, bank accounts, priorities, dreams, ambitions, and fears all have to come under the loving rule of Christ. We lay down the illusion that anything else can finally satisfy. We stop asking created things to carry the weight only Christ can bear.

And when Christ becomes our treasure, it never stays private. Families change when fathers and mothers treasure Christ more than control. Marriages change when husbands and wives treasure Christ more than winning. Churches grow strong when believers treasure Christ more than comfort, preference, recognition, or ease. The fruit we long to see together always begins with the treasure we pursue alone before God.

So the call is simple, but it's terribly painful. Hold loosely to the things of this world. Stop walking past the field day in and day out. Start digging for treasure. Because Christ is worth it.

Cricket Vs. Christ
One of the clearest modern examples of treasure-hunting faith is C. T. Studd. By the world's standards, he had everything. Born into wealth In England, he became one of the most celebrated cricket players of his day. He was a national sports star with fame, fortune, and a bright future ahead. To everyone watching, his field was already laid out before him, and he looked every bit the success.

But Studd saw a different kind of treasure. He was one of us weirdos who believed Christ was better than wealth and fame and fortune. Like the man in Jesus' parable, he gave up what others spent their lives clinging to. He gave away his wealth, left behind his fame, and walked away from the applause of the crowd. Many called him a fool, but Studd knew he had found something greater: the surpassing worth of knowing Christ.

He didn't give it all away with a long face. Joy marked C. T. Studd's sacrifice. Later, when asked about such a costly choice, Studd famously said, "If Jesus Christ be God and died for me, then no sacrifice can be too great for me to make for Him." This is how we weigh life. You do what you want to do. Everything you do is done because of your values. A diligent student studies hard not because they don't want to spend time with their friends, but because they value the higher grade more than the temporal benefit of hanging out. Who you are today, the choices you've made, for better or worse is in truth a result of the values you've held.

It's not that C. T. Studd made every right decision and that's why the Lord blessed him. If we could sit down and talk with Mr. Studd, we'd find out what we'd find with every honest Christian: regrets, missteps, foolish decisions, and mercy. He wasn't a super-Christian. He was a sinner who saw Christ as supremely valuable. That's the difference between a man like Studd and John Smith. Sorry to all the John Smiths out there. I'm not picking on you. You're not a nobody. Your name made it into my little book, so if anything, this is your moment. But the point is this: the difference is not fame, gifting, personality, or opportunity. The difference is value. What we treasure shapes what we choose. And what we choose, over time, becomes the fruit of our lives. I'm not saying that if you value Jesus like a famous Christian, you'll become famous too. I'm saying that what you value is not a side issue. It's the soil where your life takes root and the vine from which your fruit will grow.

The long-term fruit of Studd's decision was unimaginable at the time. In 1913, Studd founded the Heart of Africa Mission, a work that would later become WEC International. Through his life and ministry, Studd helped spark missionary movements that continue to ripple through the world today. Generations later, people who never heard his name are still being reached because he saw Christ as the treasure. What began as one man sailing toward the heart of Africa has become a worldwide missionary fellowship laboring for the spread of the gospel. His sacrifice, like Mel Fisher's relentless hunt for the Atocha, looked foolish to many. But when the treasure is real, the cost is never wasted. And when the treasure is Christ, the fruit of lives changed always proves more than worth it. But hear me: treasure-hunting isn't just for missionaries or pioneers. It's for every believer who dares to say, "Christ is better," and joyfully reorders his life around him.

Let me encourage you to ask yourself this question: If someone followed me around for a week, if they watched my habits, if they heard my conversations, or if they tracked my spending and observed my priorities— what would they say I treasure most?

Field Notes

Treasure-hunting isn't a one-time act; it's a daily exchange. Every day you and I are trading something temporary for something eternal. The question is, what kind of trade are we making?

Let me challenge you this week. Deliberately swap one temporary thing for something eternal. Don't wait for a grand moment—start small, start ordinary, and start now.

Skip one purchase this week and give the money away generously.

Trade one hour of scrolling for an hour of prayer or Scripture reading.

Use one awkward moment as a chance to speak about Christ.

Serve someone in secret so that they don't know who helped.

Start a simple record. Open the notes app on your phone and create a file called FIELD NOTES. Every time you make one of these exchanges, jot it down. Write a sentence like this:

"Today I am selling ___________ so I can treasure Christ more deeply."

Over time, that note will grow into your personal treasure map. It'll be a testimony of trades that seemed small in the moment but will echo forever in eternity. This is a record for yourself, so that when things get hard or sacrifices become more costly, you can be reminded that this is just another one of those things you're trading for Christ's sake.

A Final Word

You're standing on a field that contains untold treasures underneath. To the world, it looks like nothing more than dirt—ordinary, unimpressive, and definitely not worth the price. But beneath the surface lies Christ himself, hidden from eyes that cannot see, yet revealed to you by his grace.

The question is not whether the treasure is real. The question is whether you will trade for it with joy. Will you gladly sell all, releasing the clinking coins of comfort and control, or will you clutch them until they slip through your fingers? The field is before you. The treasure is waiting. The hunt has begun.

CHAPTER TWO

READING THE MAP

Mel Fisher didn't find the Atocha by luck. He found it by research. Before ever diving, he studied Spanish shipping records, old maritime charts, and archival manifests in Seville, Spain. Those documents detailed the 1622 fleet's route, the cargo aboard each ship, and where the storms had likely driven them off course. From those clues, Fisher began plotting probable sites on his own maps.

As dives began, the evidence came in fragments. In 1973, his team recovered silver bars whose weight and serial numbers matched the Atocha's recorded manifest. Two years later, they found five bronze cannons whose markings confirmed they were closing in. These discoveries weren't accidents—they were confirmations that his map was right.

Fisher's success came from knowing where to look and trusting the map enough to keep returning to it. He studied, he marked, he searched, and he stayed the course until the evidence aligned. Every treasure hunter begins not by guessing, but by learning to read the map. For believers, that map is the Word of God. It tells us where to look for Christ, how to recognize Him when we find Him, and how to keep searching when the waters seem empty.

Proverbs 2:1-5

"My son, if you receive my words and treasure up my commandments with you, making your ear attentive to wisdom and inclining your heart to understanding; yes, if you call out for insight and raise your voice for understanding, if you seek it like silver and search for it as for hidden treasures, then you will understand the fear of the LORD and find the knowledge of God."

The book of Proverbs opens with a father speaking to his son. These early chapters are not meant merely to inform the mind of the reader, but to train the heart. Each time we read the phrase "my son," we should read it as though the writer is becoming our own personal tutor, pulling us closer and whispering something precious in our ear.

My dad used to tell me a man has two options. He can be smart and learn from his mistakes, or he can be wise and learn from others. I've done both. I've also taken the third and far less impressive option, being dumb and learning from no one. But the longer I live, the more I see how much mercy there is in being warned before the damage is done. Wisdom lets you borrow the bruises of another man without having to earn every one yourself. And if that's true when listening to an earthly father, how much more when listening to the wisdom God has preserved for us in Proverbs? The wisest person is not merely the one who learns from experience. The wisest person is the one who receives the words of the Lord.

"Receive my words." The Hebrew term translated as "receive" carries the idea of taking something into your possession, not just hearing it. It's the language of a welcoming embrace. Wisdom must be received as one receives a gift, not glanced at or glossed over like passing advice. Advice or opinions are dangerous because not all advice is wisdom. Some advice is just a person handing you the leftovers of their own experience and calling it dinner. Sometimes it helps. Sometimes it doesn't. Sometimes it comes from someone who loves you but doesn't understand your life. Sometimes it comes from someone who understands your life but doesn't love you enough to tell you the whole truth. And sometimes advice has less to do with what's true and more to do with what the advice-giver values. God's Word is always true and born from a heart that infinitely loves you.

We all live inside our own heads more than we realize. Psychologists call one version of this the spotlight effect. It's the tendency to think other people are noticing us far more than they actually are. You walk into a room convinced everyone noticed your shirt, your comment, your awkward laugh, or the fact that you suddenly forgot what hands are supposed to do. In reality, most people are busy wondering whether everyone noticed their shirt, their comment, their awkward laugh, and their own weird hands. The room is full of people starring in their own little dramas, and you barely got a speaking role.

That little truth can help you relax at a party, but it also teaches us something about human advice. Much of what people tell us is filtered through their own fears, regrets, preferences, assumptions, and little internal dramas. That doesn't mean human advice is useless. God often uses faithful people to help us see clearly.

But it does mean we must learn the difference between someone's opinion and God's wisdom. The person worth trusting is the one who takes you to the Word of God and helps you hear what the Lord has said. Anecdotal advice can be helpful. A life lesson can be useful. A good story can save you from stepping into a hole someone else already fell into. But the greatest wisdom doesn't come from one person's life lived. It comes from the Lord and His Word.

"Treasure up my commandments." The word treasure comes from a root term that means to hide something. It carries the connotation of storing or guarding something of great value. This is deliberately storing away truth as if hiding gold in a safe place, not just memorizing Scripture passages. Wisdom isn't some surface-level knowledge; it's something buried deep. Proverbs 25:2 might give us a little more depth as to what Solomon meant here: "It is the glory of God to conceal things, but the glory of kings is to search things out."

The point is not that God has hidden truth at the bottom of a mine and then left us to stumble around in the dark while He watches from heaven with a grin. God isn't playing games with His creatures. He's not hiding wisdom because He's stingy. He's teaching us that truth must be pursued. Yes, wisdom is often buried deep, but the digging is part of the gift. The searching, the diligence, the sweat, the frustration, the prayer, the slow discovery: all of that shapes us. God could drop every answer into our laps fully formed, but He often chooses instead to make us search, because the search does something to us. The path matters. The digging matters.

The pursuit of wisdom is not just how we find the nugget. It's part of how God makes us into the kind of people who know what to do with it once we have it.

God's not only concerned with the outcome. If He were, wouldn't He just make us instantly complete the moment we believed? Why leave us here in this body of flesh with the same old struggles, temptations, confusion, and pain? Because the road to wisdom is part of the work of wisdom. The Lord doesn't merely hand us information. He forms us as we seek Him. The digging, the unearthing, the wrestling, the returning again and again to His Word: this is how knowledge becomes wisdom. Not because we discovered something God was unwilling to give, but because in the search, God is training our hearts to treasure what He has spoken.

"Making your ear attentive to wisdom and inclining your heart to understanding." The verbs here are active, showing what sort of posture we as sons and daughters are to have. To make the ear attentive is literally to bend the ear. This is an image of focus and eagerness. To incline the heart is to lean one's inner being toward discernment. The pursuit of wisdom begins not just with discovery but also with posture. The student bends low to hear.

That kind of posture requires humility. And I'll be honest, I've often confused humility with lowliness. Lowliness is part of humility. Pliability is part of humility. But they're not the whole thing. Sometimes I've been pliable and called it humble when really I was just unsure, timid, or afraid to stand up straight. Biblical humility is not merely thinking less of yourself. It's seeing yourself in the light of heaven. It's knowing who you are before God, both apart from Christ and now in Christ.

For a long time, I think I lived with a functionally graceless gospel. Oh, there was mercy in it. Plenty of mercy. I knew I deserved death and hell. I knew I could not save myself. I knew that left to myself, I would be the worst sinner the world had ever seen. I knew mercy meant not getting what I justly deserved. But the gospel isn't only mercy. It's also grace. Mercy means I'm spared what I deserve. Grace means I'm given what I never could have earned.

The cross didn't only atone for my sin. Through the work of Christ, I was brought into the Father's family. I'm no longer a worthless worm. And if you're in Christ, neither are you. You've been seated with Christ in heavenly places. You've been declared righteous. You've been called a child of God. You are an heir with Christ. You belong to the beloved of God.

So humility is not just seeing who you were in your sin. Humility is also seeing who you are now in Christ. That's the difference between mere pliability and biblical humility. Yes, we bow low as sinners. But we bow as sinners who have been saved, adopted, and are now being sanctified by the power of the Holy Spirit. The flesh still pulls at us. The old patterns still try to weigh us down. But we're not only what we used to be. We are new creatures in Christ. So we stay pliable before the Lord, not because we're nothing, but because He has made us His. We bend the ear, incline the heart, and search His Word with confidence because the Father is not trying to crush us. He's teaching His beloved children.

Expiation, the removal of our sin through the work of Christ, is glorious. Our guilt, shame, and rebellion are taken away. Our sins are forgiven. But if the Lord left us there, we would still be empty-handed beggars. The gospel gives more. In Christ, righteousness is counted to us. We're not only cleansed. We're also clothed. We are not only forgiven. We're also received. We are set apart as the people of God, kings and priests unto Him. Humility does not say, "I am nothing but a wretch." Humility says, "Christ alone has taken this wretch and made him someone for something far greater than himself."

When we search the Scriptures humbly, we aren't crawling toward God as if He might still despise us. We're leaning in as beloved children, eager to see and savor more of who Christ is and what He has done in sinners turned saints like us.

Next, comes the movement from posture to pursuit: "if you call out for insight and raise your voice for understanding." The Hebrew terms here paint the picture of urgency—crying out, lifting the voice, calling aloud. Wisdom isn't found by those who are indifferent. It's sought by those who are desperate to know, those who plead for insight as if their life depends on it.

I've been afraid for my life a few times. The earliest memory I have of that kind of fear came when I was just a kid playing sharks and minnows at a public pool in Georgia one summer. My brother and I spent several weeks of summer break at my grandmother's house, just outside Athens in a little town called Watkinsville. One day, to our great delight, she took us to the public pool. The kids there started playing sharks and minnows, and one kid in particular was especially aggressive. It also just so happened that he stunk at the game. I suspect those two facts were related.

I dove off the side as one of the minnows and tried to swim underneath him. To be fair, I was probably doing this to taunt the kid. What happened next has stayed with me for decades. He reached down, grabbed my hair, and held me under the water. All he had to do was tag me, and I would have become a shark in the next round. Apparently, that was not enough for this tiny pool tyrant. He grabbed my hair and kept me under.

Panic hit me immediately. I thrashed. I kicked. I tried to pull away. If I had stayed calm, it probably would not have lasted as long. But calm is not exactly the natural response when another child has decided to baptize you unto death. I started gulping water. I felt it go down the wrong way. I began gasping for breath while still under the surface, which, as you might imagine, is a terrible place to begin gasping for breath. In that moment, I really believed my next moment might not come.

Don't be afraid. I survived.

A few seconds later, he let go of my hair, and I shot to the top of the pool. I coughed and wheezed my way to the side like a kid who had forgotten the basic mechanics of swimming and breathing at the same time. I was making enough of a scene that the lifeguard came over to see what was wrong. I couldn't speak. My eyes just searched for the little criminal who had tried to send me to glory before lunch. I know that sounds dramatic, but that's how it felt.

Then I saw him. He was being shuffled out the gate by his mom or sister or whoever had brought him there. He knew what he had done. I knew what he had done. The lifeguard did not know what he had done, which felt like a real failure in the justice system. But I still couldn't speak, so justice would never come.

As I lay there on the side of the pool, coughing, wheezing, and probably looking more heroic in my own mind than I did in real life, I remember feeling how sweet air was. Just air. Ordinary air. The thing I had been breathing all day without thinking about it suddenly felt like the greatest treasure in the world. When I was under that water, I did not casually prefer air. I did not mildly appreciate air. I wanted air. I needed air. I was desperate for air.

That's the kind of urgency Solomon is describing. Not a polite interest in wisdom. Not a casual nod toward understanding. A cry. A reach. A desperate raising of the voice because life depends on it. As I fought to reach the surface, desperate to breathe again, so we are called to seek the wisdom of God. And if air is sweet to the lungs of a drowning little minnow, how much sweeter is Christ, the true life-giver, to the soul that knows it cannot live without Him.

Solomon adds this comparison, "if you seek it like silver and search for it as for hidden treasures." The verbs seek (baqash) and search (chaphas) intensify the image. One is the steady pursuit of something precious; the other is the excavation of what lies buried. Together, they picture a miner digging through rock to uncover hidden wealth. This is deliberate. The silver and treasure metaphors tell us that wisdom will not be found lying on the surface. It requires sweat and it requires persistence. We must stop worshiping the idol of comfort and start to dig for treasure, even when it hurts.

"Then you will understand the fear of the LORD and find the knowledge of God." This is the glorious purpose of this treasure hunting. The fear of the LORD is the reverent awe and moral orientation that defined biblical wisdom. It shouldn't always be terror, but rather a rightful recognition of God's holiness and authority and our position before him. If we're outside of Christ, then this fear is a terror. For those who have repented of their sins, trust in the substitutionary atonement of Christ, and are therefore beloved by the Father, reverence becomes the fuel for our obedience. Because He loves us so much, we couldn't imagine chasing after anything else.

Keep My Commandments
True wisdom isn't some abstract concept, it's the lived-out understanding of God. And what's the treasure map? The Word of God. So, receive it, value it, incline yourself to it, call out for it, seek it, search for it. All of these are active verbs that tell us treasure hunting is a journey through the Scriptures. And the destination isn't just theological insight, but obedience.

We're called to learn and grow in our understanding of the Lord. Every Sunday, we should leave the pew, the chair, or wherever we happen to be sitting with a deeper understanding of who God is and what He's said. But our churches should never become little seminaries. The sanctuary is not merely a lecture hall where truth is handed out in bite-size pieces and everyone takes notes like there'll be a quiz later. There is teaching, yes. There must be teaching. But the goal is not information alone. The goal is formation. The goal is worship. The goal is obedience. In some ways, church should feel less like sitting in a classroom and more like being invited onto the field.

I love the Chicago Cubs. Let me correct that. My wife and I love the Chicago Cubs, and therefore our children are expected to love the Chicago Cubs. That's just how family discipleship works. We recently got back from our first trip to Wrigley Field, where we watched the Cubs lose two games, which felt spiritually formative in its own way. But one of the most memorable moments came before the game even started. We arrived early, climbed up to our nosebleed seats, and from the top of the stadium I could see the whole ground crew working feverishly to prepare the field.

Every step seemed timed. Every movement had rhythm. Everyone knew where to go and what to do. At one point, they brought a fan down onto the field and gave him the special experience of helping chalk the foul lines and carry the water hose while the head groundskeeper sprayed down the dirt. They explained what to do. They showed him how to do it. They put the tools in his hands and gave him the direction he needed. And from the very top of Wrigley Field, I could see his smile. He was grinning from ear to ear, sweating in the Chicago sun, helping prepare the field for the game. And it occurred to me: that's a picture of worshipful discipleship.

That's what the "pregame" of the Christian life should look like in the church. We're not merely trying to fill people's heads with correct answers. We're training saints to step onto the field. We're teaching them what the Lord has said, showing them how to walk in it, putting tools in their hands, and helping them learn the joy of obedience. Knowledge is needed. Absolutely. Don't get the foul line wrong. Heaven knows the umpires need all the help they can get. But knowledge without love, without joy, without worship, without obedience, is not the wisdom Proverbs is calling us to pursue.

This is why Jesus said, "If you love me, you will keep my commandments" (John 14:15). Obedience isn't the proof of our strength. It's the fruit of our affection. Christ never separates love from obedience because both flow from the same heart. When we obey the Word, we're not trying to earn the Lord's favor or impress Him with our discipline. We're living out devotion. Obedience is love with work gloves on. It's affection that has learned where to put its feet.

Through His commands, God reveals what He values and therefore invites us to treasure those same things. Each command becomes a window into God's heart. To obey them is to love what He loves, to walk the path where He walks, to see the world as He sees it. And in that walking, we find the treasure itself, which is Christ formed in us.

Not My Own Will

The treasure is Christ Himself, and obedience is how we reach out and lay hold of Him. Every command of Scripture is a pathway to deeper communion with Jesus. Each act of obedience, done from a heart of love, is like brushing away the sand from buried treasure.

We often think of obedience as the price we pay to find God's favor, but the Scriptures teach the exact opposite. Obedience is a grace-enabled ability to live in harmony with God's will. It's what happens when the words we've "received" and "treasured up" begin to mold our desires as well as our actions. Obedience is not a transaction but the means by which we hold the treasure because, in obedience, we hold Christ closer and closer.

The greatest obstacle between me and obedience is not usually confusion. It's not that I have no idea what God has said. It's that I know what He's said, and something in me still wants to argue. I want Christ, yes, but I also want comfort. I want holiness, but I also want ease. I want wisdom, but I also want to be right. I want treasure in heaven, but I also have a strange affection for the shiny little trinkets I can hold in my hand right now.

That's why obedience is never merely about behavior. It's about worship. Every act of obedience asks the same question: What do you treasure most? When God says forgive, the question is not only, "Will I forgive?" It's also, "Do I treasure Christ more than my right to be angry?" When God says give, the question is not only, "Will I give?" It's, "Do I treasure Christ more than money?" When God says flee sin, the question is not only, "Will I stop?" It's also, "Do I treasure Christ more than the pleasure this sin promises me?"

Jesus said that He came not to do His own will, but the will of the Father who sent Him (John 6:38). He treasured the Father above all else, so every word He spoke, every miracle He performed, every step He took was governed by delight in His Father's will. Jesus perfectly models the life we're called to live by the kind of obedience He showed us. His obedience was not mechanical; it was relational. He obeyed because He loved.

And nowhere do we see this more clearly than in the garden. On the night before the cross, Jesus prayed, "Not my will, but yours, be done." That wasn't the prayer of a man who found obedience easy. That was the prayer of the obedient Son who felt the full weight of what obedience would cost. He wasn't strolling casually toward suffering. He was sweating drops of blood. And still, He surrendered. Not because pain was pleasant. But because the Father's will was better, and the joy set before Him was greater.

We're not stronger than our desires. We're not naturally brave treasure hunters with lanterns in our hands and a perfect sense of direction. Most of the time, we're more like nervous children holding a plastic shovel, hoping the map isn't asking us to dig somewhere uncomfortable. But Christ doesn't merely hand us commands and tell us to try harder. He gives us Himself. He gives us His Spirit. He teaches us to pray, "Not my will, but Yours, be done," and then He gives us grace to mean it.

In the same way, we don't obey to earn Christ; we obey because we already have Him. The commands of God are not barriers to joy. Each command that we find and treasure is a point plotted on the map that leads us into deeper fellowship with Jesus. When we receive His Word and treasure it, when we incline our hearts toward it and seek it like hidden treasure, what we're really doing is learning to love what He loves and to walk as He walked.

Not By Accident
Solomon describes obedience as listening, leaning in, calling out, seeking after, and searching diligently. Every one of those is active. None of them happen by accident. Nobody drifts into treasure hunting. Nobody accidentally becomes the kind of person who receives the Word, treasures it, bends the ear, inclines the heart, and searches for wisdom like silver. That kind of life is intentional. It means you have set your heart on finding Christ in the ordinary commands of Scripture.

I have good news for you: the treasure is not hidden beyond reach. God has not buried obedience beneath a thousand feet of theological granite and then handed us a plastic spoon. Most of the time, knowing what we're called to do is not the hard part. The hard part is doing it with Christ in mind. The hard part is seeing the command not as a cold rule, but as a marked place on the map where fellowship with Jesus can be found.

When you forgive someone who doesn't deserve it, you're holding the treasure.

When you serve without recognition, you're holding the treasure.

When you trust the Lord's providence in the middle of uncertainty, you're holding the treasure.

When you open the Word and obey what you find there, you're holding onto Jesus as tightly as you could a bar of gold.

Every act of obedience, whether small or large, becomes another step along the path. The treasure is not that obedience earns us something separate from Christ. The treasure is that obedience draws us nearer to Christ Himself. The joy of the hunt is not just knowing the map. It's walking the path the map lays out for us and discovering that the Lord is with us in every step.

When my son turned ten, we made him a treasure map. It covered a huge sheet of paper, with little drawings marking each stop along the way. Every clue led to something he loved: donuts for breakfast, subs for lunch, and the final X marked the day's big surprise, go-karts. We could have just told him the plan. We could have said, "Hey buddy, today we're getting donuts, eating subs, and going to ride go-karts." He would have loved that. But letting him follow the map made the whole journey come alive.

He studied each stop. He made his guesses. He tried to figure out what each clue meant. And with overwhelming excitement, he led the way. The map didn't replace the gifts. It led him into the joy of them. At the end of the day, we didn't just talk about where we ended up. We talked about the path. We talked about the clues. We talked about the fun of discovering what had been planned for him all along.
This is one of the gifts the Lord has given us in His Word. He's not merely told us there is treasure somewhere out there and then left us wandering around, hoping we trip

over it. He's given us the map. He's marked the path. He's told us where to walk, what to avoid, what to seek, what to love, what to put to death, and what to hold fast. His commands are not random obstacles scattered across the Christian life to prove whether we are serious enough. They're the Father's loving directions for His children.

The journey of following the map will take us through the valley of the shadow of death. It will lead us through hard commands, costly forgiveness, quiet faithfulness, and moments when obedience feels like digging through rock with a spork. But the end is not merely a hopeful possibility. It's a guarantee. One day, when the hunt is over and faith becomes sight, we will see that every faithful step was never wasted. Every "yes" to God's command was not another payment made toward the treasure, but another moment of holding Christ more tightly. Every time we chose faithfulness over comfort, we were not earning Him. We were learning Him. We were learning His heart, His ways, His beauty, and His worth.

Obedience is not the price of the treasure, it's the proof that we have already found Him. And the more we obey, the more clearly we see that the treasure was never merely at the end of the path. He was with us on every step of the hunt.

Field Notes
This week, treat the Word of God like your treasure map.
Before you open your Bible, ask the Lord to show you
one command or truth to obey that day. When you find
it, stop. Don't rush to the next verse. Write it down, pray
over it, and live it out, as it is the next point on the map.

Maybe it's forgiving someone.
Maybe it's resisting a familiar temptation, or choosing
patience instead of frustration.

Whatever it is, obey it joyfully, knowing that obedience
itself is how you hold the true treasure of nearness to
Jesus.

Write it in the journal you've started titled FIELD NOTES:

"Today I followed the map by obeying ________________,
because I trust that obedience draws me closer to
Christ."

Let this become your pattern. The more you follow the
map, the closer you get to your reward.

A Final Word
Every treasure hunter needs a map, and God has given
us one. His Word doesn't merely tell us about the
treasure—it leads us to it. Every time we obey, we're
walking one line closer to Christ.

And what a great promise we have: the map will never
fail you, because the One who drew it walks beside you.
Keep reading. Keep following. The treasure is yours for
the taking.

CHAPTER THREE

TREASURES IN HEAVEN

The Spanish ship known as the Atocha went down in a hurricane off the coast of Florida in 1622. For 363 years, her treasure lay hidden beneath the sea until Mel Fisher and his crew finally found the mother lode in 1985.

But the Atocha was not the only ship that went down in that storm. Her sister ship, the Santa Margarita, sank with her. And from that same world of Spanish gold, wrecked ships, and treasure pulled from the ocean floor came one particularly famous piece: Gold Bar 27.

Gold Bar 27 weighed 74.85 ounces, nearly five pounds of solid gold, and was valued at more than half a million dollars. The bar was placed on display at the Mel Fisher Maritime Heritage Museum in Key West. But this was not one of those museum pieces sitting far away behind glass while a security guard silently judged you for breathing too close to it. The museum had built a special plexiglass case so visitors could reach in and lift it. They could touch gold from the 1600s. They could hold treasure that had spent centuries buried beneath waves, storms, sand, and silence. They could literally feel the weight of history in their hands.

Then, on August 18, 2010, in broad daylight, two men walked into the museum and pulled off one of the boldest treasure heists in recent memory. With shocking ease, they slipped Gold Bar 27 out of its case and disappeared into the streets of Key West. Think about that. This bar had survived a hurricane that sank ships, hundreds of years under the sea, discovery by treasure hunters, preservation, display, and even the long strange journey from the ocean floor into a museum case. And then, in just a few moments, it was gone.

The thieves later cut the bar into pieces and sold it off bit by bit. When they were finally caught and sentenced in 2018, investigators had recovered only one small fragment, about three percent of the original bar. The rest, once thought safe, once held by millions of hands, once placed where everyone could admire it, had been scattered and lost.

That's the part that gets me.

Not that men stole gold. Men have been stealing gold for as long as men have loved gold. What gets me is that something so valuable could be held, admired, displayed, guarded, and still be lost. A thing can be precious and still be stolen. A treasure can be real and still slip through human hands.

Matthew 6:19-21
"Do not lay up for yourselves treasures on earth, where moth and rust destroy and where thieves break in and steal." If you wanted a living picture of Jesus' words in Matthew 6, this was it. Even the mosts secure items behind museum glass can vanish in a heartbeat. Earthly treasures, no matter how impressive, are never safe for long.

The first thing we see in Matthew 6 is a command. "Do not lay up for yourselves treasures on earth." The phrase "lay up" comes from a Greek term that means to stockpile, to heap up, or to build a treasury. It speaks of something intentional. Nobody drifts into the kind of treasure storage Jesus is talking about. You choose what you gather, and you decide where to keep it. Jesus isn't just warning against having possessions; He's warning against constructing your life around a vault that won't last. What's more, He's issuing a command— do not store up earthly treasures.

This passage has sometimes been used by well-meaning Christians to warn against gaining wealth, owning property, enjoying nice things, or building a comfortable life. Pair it with Paul's instruction to "aspire to live quietly" and "work with your hands" in 1 Thessalonians 4:11–12, and some have concluded that the godly life must be as plain and possessionless as possible. Now, I am not saying we all need to go buy Bentleys and shop at Louis Vuitton. That would be its own kind of ridiculous. But the opposite error is still an error. Jesus is not commanding Christians to take a vow of poverty. He's commanding us to treasure the right things.

If I go to work every day so I can feed my family well, provide a comfortable home, care for their needs, and store away resources that may one day bless my children and grandchildren, that's not ungodly. That is good stewardship. Scripture does not condemn a man for providing for his household. In fact, Proverbs 13:22 says, "A good man leaves an inheritance to his children's children, but the sinner's wealth is laid up for the righteous."

Notice that Solomon doesn't merely say a good man feeds his children today. He says a good man leaves an inheritance to his children's children. That means he thinks beyond himself. He thinks beyond the moment. He works, plans, saves, builds, and stores in a way that blesses people who will come after him. I don't know about you, but that takes effort. That takes wisdom. That takes a kind of storing up.

So Jesus is not contradicting Solomon, He's not warning us that every savings account is sin or every nice thing is a spiritual trap. He's taking us deeper, way deeper than that. He's warning us about misplaced treasure. He's confronting the kind of heart that takes earthly goods, even good earthly goods, and builds its hope there. There's a world of difference between using wealth faithfully and trusting wealth foolishly. One is stewardship. The other is worship.

Jesus could have just given a command, and that should settle it. Instead, He graciously lists for us the enemies we're up against: "where moth and rust destroy." In the ancient world, wealth wasn't just coins; it also included fine garments, textiles, and stored grain. Moths could eat through the most elegant robes. Rust (literally "eating" in Greek) would corrode precious metals or spoil food. The point was clear: no matter how carefully you guard earthly goods, time itself is against you. All that glitters eventually fades.

Time and the natural order of things aren't your only enemies: "where thieves break in and steal." The word for "break in" literally means "to dig through." In His day, houses were often made of clay or mud brick, and thieves would dig straight through the walls at night to steal whatever was stored inside. You can build your vault, you can set your guards, but what you prize most can still be snatched away in a moment.

By contrast, Jesus gives the alternative. "But lay up for yourselves treasures in heaven." Store them where no moth can eat, no rust can decay, and where no thief can dig through. Heaven's vault cannot be broken. What is truly kept there is untouchable by time, the natural order of things, and sinful hands. But we have to be careful here. Jesus isn't merely telling us to move our greed to a safer location. Heaven isn't just earth with better locks.

We should be honest. Some of us grew up singing more about mansions in glory than we sang about Christ Himself. And look, I'm not against mansions. If the Lord wants to hand me keys to a place that doesn't need repairs, mold remediation, or a new roof every ten years, I'll receive it with joy. But the mansion is not the treasure. Christ is.

The crown is not the treasure. Christ is.
The streets of gold are not the treasure. Christ is.
The reunion with loved ones, as sweet as that will be, is not the treasure. Christ is.

Heaven is not glorious because the real estate's better. Heaven is glorious because Jesus is there. Every lesser promise of heaven gets its beauty from Him. The mansion is wonderful because it's the Father's house. The crown is wonderful because we will cast it before the Lamb. The streets of gold are wonderful because they lead us to the feet of the King. The absence of pain is wonderful because nothing will ever again hinder our joy in Him. Even the wiping away of every tear is precious because it is God Himself who wipes them away.

So when Jesus says, "Lay up for yourselves treasures in heaven," He's not telling us to be religious now so we can get nicer stuff later. He's calling us to build our lives around what cannot be separated from Him. Heavenly treasure is heavenly because Christ is there. Heaven's vault is not secure merely because the locks are better. It's secure because the treasure is bound up in the eternal God who cannot decay, who fail, and who cannot be taken from us.

And this is where Jesus presses deeper than our wallets, our houses, our bank accounts, or any of our possessions. He goes after our hearts: "For where your treasure is, there your heart will be also."

Gravitational Forces
Earthly treasures are fragile. No matter how tightly we grip them, they slip through our fingers. Time corrodes, decay consumes, and thieves scheme. Jesus doesn't speak as if these things might happen; He declares they will. That's the built-in law of this world. Everything here eventually breaks, everything rots, everything dies.

Heavenly treasures, however, are eternal. When Jesus calls us to "lay up treasures in heaven," He's not offering spiritual poetry. He's describing a reality: a heavenly vault that's guarded by the power of God. What's deposited there is truly safe.

Security, therefore, is not found in what we can see or hold. This is such a huge lesson that we have to learn over and over again. Earth offers us countless forms of false security, none of which can withstand the forces of time or loss. True security rests only in Christ, who secures our eternal inheritance. This is what Peter describes as "imperishable, undefiled, and unfading, kept in heaven for you" (1 Peter 1:4).

And so with that said, let me say this; what you treasure determines your direction. Jesus says, "Where your treasure is, there your heart will be also." We often think it works the other way. We often think that our heart sets our treasure. Jesus flips that. Your treasure pulls your heart like gravity. Where you invest your money, your time, your affections—that's where your heart will follow. I implore you, understand this spiritual law of gravity. Don't wait for your heart to be pulled toward obedience. Be obedient, and then watch your heart follow that treasure like the moon follows the earth.

This is why a believer's portfolio isn't measured by what we own but by how we obey Christ. It's measured in love, in generosity, and in gospel-focused work. Those are the deposits that will endure. Everything else eventually falls apart. The Christian's job is to keep finding more and more of our satisfaction in Christ alone. God never meant for us to be satisfied with what this world can give anyway.

We often wait to obey until our hearts feel ready. We wait to forgive until we feel like forgiving. We wait to give until we feel generous. We wait to serve until we feel excited. We wait to open the Word until we feel hungry.

But Jesus teaches us that the heart follows the treasure. Put your treasure in the right place, and your heart will begin to feel the pull.

This doesn't mean obedience is fake until the feeling shows up. it means obedience is one of the ways God trains our affections. A man who gives generously is not merely moving money. He's loosening the grip of greed. A woman who serves quietly is not merely completing a task. She's storing treasure where applause cannot reach. A believer who opens the Word day after day is not merely checking off a discipline. He's placing his heart under the steady gravity of Christ.

Our loves are not as fixed as we think they are. They're trained. They're aimed. They're strengthened by repetition. The more we invest in earthly things as ultimate, the heavier their pull becomes. The more we invest in the kingdom, the more our hearts learn to feel the weight of eternity. This is the call of discipleship. This is how the Spirit uses ordinary obedience to teach us what's truly precious.

Spiritual Audit
If it's true that treasures pull the heart like gravity, then the question is no longer abstract; the question must be personal. Where am I making my deposits? Think of it like a spiritual audit.

What consumes my energy?

What consumes my money and my passion?

If the ledger of my life were opened before Christ, would it show heaven as my bank, or earth?

There are at least three arenas where this audit becomes painfully clear. And just like before pull out a pen and a scrap of paper. Don't just read through this page is if it were any of the other pages in the book. Seriously put the book down and actually write something down. I know you, you're thinking "eh I'll do it later..." You won't. I never do.

Ok, I don't really know you. But I kinda do.

Money: *Generosity vs. Greed*
Our statements say more about our theology than we realize. Every dollar spent is either clutched as if it were ultimate or released as if Christ were ultimate. Where does my money flow? What is my money for? Is it for myself, or for the work of Christ?

Time: *Eternal vs. Trivial*
We all receive the same twenty-four hours, but not all hours are equal in weight. How much of my week is absorbed by what vanishes at death, compared to what carries into eternity?

Affections: *Holy vs. Hollow*
This is the deepest vault of all. Where does my mind wander when nothing is demanding it? Where does my heart rest when it's free to choose? What I daydream about reveals what I delight in. And what I delight in is my treasure.

If you conduct this kind of audit honestly, you'll grow. You will begin to see what has been pulling your heart. Earth's vaults may look full, but treasure that can decay is already fading. Heaven's vault holds what is kept for Christ's glory.

See. Aren't you glad you went and got that pencil and
wrote the answers down?

Field Notes

This week, choose one investment to make in heaven's vault. Don't spread yourself thin—pick just one and pour into it with intention.

- Maybe it's giving quietly to someone who would never expect it.
- Maybe it's volunteering where no spotlight shines.
- Maybe it's setting aside time to encourage a weary believer.

Write it down in your FIELD NOTES:
"This week I will move treasure from earth to heaven by __________."

Let that line be more than words. Let it be your deposit slip into heaven's account.

A Final Word

Chasing earthly treasure is like chasing shadows. It looks solid until you reach for it, and then it slips through your fingers. But heavenly treasure is as solid as Christ Himself—unbreakable and everlasting. Every deposit into His vault is secure.

Don't waste your hunt on what can vanish. Store treasure where it will never fade. Anchor your heart in heaven. The treasure is real. The vault is secure. And the joy of the hunt is only just beginning.

CHAPTER FOUR

CROWDED WATERS

You can only imagine that spending sixteen years diving in the same stretch of ocean might draw some attention. Mel Fisher knew what it was like to have crowded waters. Over time, word spread about the elusive treasure of the Atocha, and soon his once-lonely hunt became a busy sea. Other divers appeared—some seasoned, some novice, some simply curious. A few came ready to work, others wanted to watch, and more than a few were simply in the way.

But Fisher wasn't known for pushing people out. He welcomed anyone who wanted to help, though he was always honest about what the work would cost. The job paid little. He could only afford minimum wage until the treasure was found. That kind of truthfulness quickly sorted the dreamers from the devoted. Some stayed, believing the treasure was worth the wait. Others left, unwilling to labor that long for something they couldn't see yet. Still others tried to launch their own hunts, only to fail soon after.

That's what it means to search for real treasure. The longer you stay in the waters, the more crowded it gets. But what separates the true hunter from the casual swimmer isn't how fast they find it, but how faithfully they stay the course when others drift away.

Colossians 3:12-14

"Put on then, as God's chosen ones, holy and beloved, compassionate hearts, kindness, humility, meekness, and patience, bearing with one another and, if one has a complaint against another, forgiving each other; as the Lord has forgiven you, so you also must forgive. And above all these put on love, which binds everything together in perfect harmony."

The phrase "put on" comes from the Greek word meaning to clothe oneself or dress deliberately for a purpose. Paul continues the imagery he began earlier in the chapter. Believers have taken off the "old self" and now must put on the "new." This is intentional language. You don't drift into the wardrobe of Christ, you choose what to wear. Before giving a single command, Paul reminds his readers who they are. "Chosen" points to God's initiative in salvation. "Holy" means set apart for His use. And "beloved" speaks of a settled, covenant love. The command we're about to see rests on this foundation of identity. We clothe ourselves in these virtues because we already belong to Christ. And this is always how the Lord issues commands. The imperative, or the command, comes because of the indicative, or the declaration of who we are in Jesus.

It's impossible to do what the Lord has commanded us apart from Christ. I mean that plainly. It's impossible to love people the way we're called to love them if all we have is our own natural strength. It seems like every Christian wedding I've attended or officiated has included a reading from 1 Corinthians 13. And don't get me wrong, 1 Corinthians 13 is beautiful. It's also ridiculous. Not ridiculous because it is wrong, but because it exposes how far beyond us real love is. "Love bears all things"? Tell me how that's going when your husband walks through the door holding the keys to a new boat you two never discussed. "Love believes all things"? Sure. "But honey, I saved so much money by buying all these things on sale." That's a sentence that has started more marital sanctification than almost anything else on earth.

That's the point. The love Scripture describes is heavenly, not earthly. The kind of compassion, kindness, humility, meekness, patience, and forgiveness Paul is about to command does not come naturally to us. The natural man may be polite. He may be agreeable. He may even be nice when the coffee is strong, the bills are paid, the children are quiet, and nobody has offended him in the last forty-five minutes. But biblical love is something deeper. It's love that bears with real sinners, forgives real wrongs, and stays tender in the crowded waters of church life.

That's why Scripture so often reminds us who we are in Christ before telling us how to live. God doesn't hand us impossible commands and then stand back with crossed arms to see whether we can pull it off. He tells us what He has made us. Chosen. Holy. Beloved. Then He says, "Now put on what fits." You cannot obey these commands in your own strength. You obey them as one who belongs to Christ, depends on Christ, and is being remade by Christ. These garments are not costumes for religious people pretending to be better than they are. They're the wardrobe of the new self, given to those who have been raised with Christ.

Paul begins naming the garments, and none of them are meant for display. They're meant for actual people, which is deeply unfortunate, because actual people are where my godliness starts running into problems. Nobody needs patience sitting alone in a silent room. I can be meek when no one's pushing me. I can be humble when no one's questioning me. And I can be kind when nobody's being difficult. It's amazing how godly I can feel when no actual people are involved.

"Compassionate hearts," or literally, "bowels of mercy." It sounds strange to us, but the image is powerful. This isn't distant pity. This is mercy felt deep down. It's the kind of compassion that doesn't look at a struggling brother or sister and immediately ask, "Why aren't they over this yet?" It sees weakness and moves toward it. It sees sorrow and doesn't become annoyed by it. Compassion is the garment that keeps us from becoming cold in those crowded waters.

Then Paul adds kindness, which could be defined as, goodness with gentleness in its hands. It's not just being nice, which is often nothing more than avoiding conflict with a pleasant face. Kindness does good. It speaks carefully. It helps practically. It enters the room without making the room heavier. In the church, kindness matters because truth can become sharp in our hands. Some people are right in the same way a hammer is right about every nail it comes in contact with. It's accurate, maybe, but not always helpful. I'm not saying that kindness weakens truth. It just makes truth easier to receive.

Humility is a lowliness of mind, or seeing yourself rightly before God and others. It's not pretending you have nothing to offer. It's not walking around like a sad balloon with all the air let out. Humility remembers that whatever wisdom, strength, gifting, or maturity you have was given to you. You didn't manufacture grace. You received it. And once you know that, it becomes much harder to look down on the person who's still learning what God has already taught you.

Meekness is often confused for weakness, but really meekness requires untold strength, under control. It's the man who could win the argument but chooses to shepherd the conversation instead. It is the woman who could embarrass someone with what she knows but chooses to build them up instead. Meekness matters because strong people are dangerous when they are not gentle. Strong opinions, strong personalities, strong convictions, strong gifts—all of them need to be clothed in meekness, or they will bruise the very people they were meant to help.

Patience, Paul continues, is calm long-suffering. It's endurance that refuses to retaliate. It's what you need when growth is slow, when conversations repeat, when the same weakness shows up again, and when someone's sanctification seems to be moving at the speed of a government office. Patience doesn't mean pretending sin is fine. It means refusing to become harsh because change might be slow. The Lord has been patient with us, and in the church He teaches us to wear that same patience toward one another.

These are not decorative garments, they aren't spiritual accessories we put on so we look more mature than we are. They're the clothes we need because following

Jesus means living close to other people who are also still being sanctified. Compassion moves toward weakness. Kindness does good gently. Humility remembers grace. Meekness restrains strength. Patience stays when the process is slow.

The phrase "bearing with" comes from a particular root term that means to hold up or endure. It carries the sense of choosing to remain rather than to withdraw. It's a picture of steady forbearance under the weight of relationships.

"If anyone has a complaint." Put another way, if anyone has an honest grievance or charge against another believer. Let's face it: Paul says "if," but we know that it's more like "when" we have an honest grievance, right? Paul tells us that when that happens we are to be "forgiving" each other. The idea from this term is to show grace or to freely grant favor. Forgiveness here isn't earned, it's extended. And before we can try to come up with our own level of forgiveness, Paul immediately gives the length of the kind of forgiveness he means: "as the Lord has forgiven you, so you also must forgive." The believer's kind of forgiveness flows from the finished work of Jesus. Our forgiveness ought to mirror or emulate the forgiveness we've received from Jesus.

Finally, and most importantly, Paul completes the outfit by saying, "And above all these put on love, which binds everything together in perfect harmony." "Love" (agapē) is not simply another virtue in the list. It's the one that holds all the others in place. The word "binds" carries the idea of a fastening bond, like ligaments holding a body together. Or if we continue our analogy, love would be the belt. "Perfect harmony" can be misunderstood. It doesn't mean everything in the church will move forward flawlessly. The idea is completeness or maturity. Love unites the garments into a single, whole, complete outfit. Without love, the others fall apart.

Paul doesn't tell us to try harder, he reminds us who we are. Chosen. Holy. Beloved. Then, and only then, he tells us what to do. The believer, already loved by God, must now be clothed in the character of Christ. These virtues are not mere moral improvements. They are not Christian manners. They are the wardrobe of the new creation. This is how people who have found the true treasure begin to live. We put on what belongs to Christ because we belong to Christ.

Dive Deeper
Paul's words here are not meant to stay folded neatly in the dresser. Compassionate hearts, kindness, humility, meekness, patience, forbearance, forgiveness, and love are meant to be worn in public. They're meant for the crowded places where real people say real things, carry real wounds, and occasionally make you wonder whether sanctification is happening at all. These are not private virtues for quiet mornings with coffee and a Bible. These are the clothes of the new self, and they are meant to be worn where people are hard to love.

Start with those who don't know Christ. The unbelieving world doesn't need Christians who are merely annoyed that sinners sin. Lost people act lost because, they're lost. Blind people stumble because they cannot see. And dead people don't need a lecture about how poorly they are acting for dead people. They need life. So when Paul tells us to put on compassionate hearts and kindness, he's giving us the right posture toward those outside of Christ. Compassion sees beneath the behavior to the need. Kindness moves toward that need with gentleness and truth.

That does't mean we pretend sin isn't sin. Kindness isn't cowardice. Compassion doesn't require us to soften what God has said. But it does change the way we carry the truth. There is a way to be right that makes the truth look ugly. There's a way to speak about sin that sounds less like grief and more like disgust. If Christ has shown mercy to us, then mercy ought to shape how we speak to those who still do not know Him. We don't proclaim the gospel from above them, as though we climbed out of the grave by our own impressive moral effort. We speak as people who were also dead until Christ made us alive.

Evangelism isn't merely a message we deliver it's also a mercy we're called to wear, or give. I guess the clothing analogy is a little weak here. But you get the point. When we answer hostility with patience, when we serve people who don't yet understand why we serve them, we're displaying the very gospel we proclaim. We're showing them, in small and imperfect ways, what kind of Savior Christ is. The world may reject the message, but let it not be because we dressed the message in pride, harshness, or impatience.

But crowded waters are not only filled with unbelievers. Sometimes the people most difficult to love are the ones sitting three rows over on Sunday morning. They believe the same gospel. They sing the same songs. They may even say "amen" at the same parts of the sermon. And then they frustrate you so deeply that you start looking up whether "bearing with one another" has an expiration date.

Paul doesn't let us escape, he says we're to bear with "one another". That means we choose to remain instead of withdraw, even with those who claim Christ. We carry the weight of relationships even when those relationships get heavy. Then he goes further. "If one has a complaint against another," we are to forgive. Not if the complaint is imaginary and not if the wound is small enough to ignore. Paul assumes there will be real grievances among real believers. Someone will sin. Someone will speak carelessly. Someone will disappoint you. Someone will fail to see how much they hurt you. It's funny how shocked we get when that happens. But when that happens, the command is not to nurse the wound until it becomes part of your personality. The command is to forgive as the Lord has forgiven you.

That phrase ruins all our favorite escape routes. "As the Lord has forgiven you." Not as they deserve. Not as quickly as they apologize. Not as fully as they understand what they did. As the Lord has forgiven you. That kind of forgiveness is impossible for the world since it's not empowered by the Spirit. That's what makes it distinctly Christian. Forgiveness is not pretending the wound never happened like the wisdom of the world offers. It's not calling evil good either. It's also not handing an unsafe person unlimited access to your life. Forgiveness means releasing the debt into the hands of the Lord because Christ has released a far greater debt from you.

And above all of this, Paul says to put on love. Love is what keeps compassion from turning into pity. Love keeps kindness from becoming mere politeness. Love keeps humility from collapsing into insecurity. Love keeps meekness from becoming weakness. Love keeps patience from becoming silent resentment. Love binds the whole outfit together, not because church life will always move in perfect peace, but because love keeps pulling the people of God toward maturity.

This is what it means to treasure Christ among others. Toward unbelievers, we wear mercy because Christ had mercy on us. Toward believers, we wear patience and forgiveness because Christ has been patient and forgiving toward us. The same gospel that saved us now teaches us how to swim in crowded waters without becoming cold, proud, bitter, or harsh. For some of us that's a massive need. I mean that in all love, but it's important to highlight. There are many of us out here forgiving others with our lips, but our hearts are far from love as the motivation. When it's hard for you to find the proper loving motivation, focus on the gospel.

We'll never move past the gospel into something deeper. Simply because there is nothing deeper than the gospel. We can move deeper into the gospel. The grace that made us chosen, holy, and beloved which is the same grace that teaches us how to love people who are lost, people who are weak, and people who wound us. This is what Paul calls us to: to put on what belongs to Christ because we belong to Christ.

Field Notes

This week, notice who's in your waters. The people who test your patience are the very ones God placed there to teach you how to love. When frustration rises, pause and remember: "as the Lord has forgiven you."

- Send a message.
- Offer help.
- Or just loosen the grip on frustration or resentment you're so tightly holding.

Write it down in your FIELD NOTES:

"Today I loved __________ in the crowded waters by __________, because I've been loved by Christ."

No real treasure is found in calm seas.

A Final Word

The hunt is rarely lonely for long. Sooner or later, the waters fill with people. People who bump, splash, and drift carelessly across your path. Don't wish them away. Love them. The same grace that found you is still at work in them. So, stay kind, stay patient. Stay anchored in the gospel. That's how treasure is found. Even, or I should say, especially—when the waters get crowded.

CHAPTER FIVE

THE JOY OF HUNTING

Treasure hunting is never easy. Mel Fisher knew that better than anyone. After years of false leads and near-ruin chasing the wreck of the Nuestra Señora de Atocha, many thought he was crazy. Storms battered his crew. Finances dried up. Still, every morning, he would rally his divers with the same words: "Today's the day."

In 1975, the hunt turned deadly. Fisher's son Dirk, his Daughter-in-law Angel, and diver Rick Gage were aboard a boat called the Northwind when disaster struck. The vessel capsized at sea, and all three drowned. The tragedy should have ended the dream, and for most men, it would have. Losing a son and daughter-in-law is the kind of loss that stops these things permanently.

But Fisher pressed on. Day after day, he returned to the water. His eyes were fixed on the treasure that still lay beneath the waves. Even the death of family could not turn him from the pursuit.

To outsiders, it looked like madness. Sheer madness driving himself and his crew through storms, danger, and even grief for the sake of what—maybe finding some gold? And yet that's the extremity of devotion that marks the greatest treasure hunts. Few pursuits ever demand so much, or cost so dearly.

Hebrews 12:2

"...looking to Jesus, the founder and perfecter of our faith, who for the joy that was set before him endured the cross, despising the shame, and is seated at the right hand of the throne of God."

The phrase "looking to Jesus"doesn't just mean "glancing."It means turning your eyes away from everything else and fixing them firmly on one object. It's the language of deliberate focus. Imagine a runner straining toward the finish line. Eyes locked forward, refusing to be distracted by the crowd, the competitors, or even his own fatigue. Nothing can deter him. That's the image. Christ is not one option among many; He is the object, He is the target, He is the treasure you fix on when all else is stripped away.

My wife was thirty-six weeks pregnant with our daughter when I fell on my motorcycle and cracked my shoulder blade. Okay, fine, it was a scooter. A Yamaha Majesty, to be exact, which is basically the minivan of motorcycles. But it was large enough to injure me, so I'm counting it.

It had just rained, and I was probably going five miles per hour when I hit a slick spot at a red light. The scooter just banana-peeled out from under me. One second I was upright, dignified, and pretending I rode a real motorcycle. The next second I was flat on my back in the road, staring at the sky, trying to decide whether my pride or my shoulder hurt worse. For the last few weeks of my wife's pregnancy and the first few weeks of my daughter's life, I was nearly useless. Not ideal timing. Apparently, newborns and very pregnant wives still need things even when dad has heroically lost a battle with damp pavement.

I was stubborn and refused the ambulance ride. I asked the firemen to call my wife instead. So I sat on the side of the road in an incredible amount of pain, waiting for my pregnant wife to come pick me up from my scooter wreck. There are moments in life when you can feel your dignity quietly packing its bags and leaving town.

As I sat there, I kept trying to figure out what went wrong. I thought back to the motorcycle endorsement class I had taken a few years earlier. One of the biggest lessons the instructor drilled into us was this: keep your eyes on the good road. When you see a pothole, gravel, debris, or some danger in the road, the natural tendency is to stare at it. But if you stare at the hazard, you tend to drift toward it. Your hands follow your eyes. Your body follows your focus. So the instructor kept telling us to look where we wanted to go.

But that day there was no pothole. No branch. No obvious hazard sitting in the road with a little sign that said, "Hello, I am here to ruin your afternoon." That's what bothered me. I didn't wreck because I was staring at the wrong thing. I wrecked because I was hardly paying attention at all. The whole road had become dangerous because I had grown casual. The rain had changed the conditions, but I rode as though nothing had changed. My focus was dull. My attention was lazy. And then, all at once, I was on my back.

Our spiritual walk can feel like that. Sometimes we find ourselves sitting on the side of the proverbial road, wounded, confused, and trying to figure out what obvious danger we hit. But the problem isn't always one big pothole. Sometimes it's a long, slow loss of focus.

Sometimes it's apathy. Sometimes it's a dullness of heart that causes us to stop looking carefully at Christ and start coasting through conditions that require our attention.

Looking to Jesus is not only about avoiding obvious holes in the road. It's about refusing to let the heart grow casual. It's maintaining a fierce gaze on Christ when the road is wet, when nothing dramatic seems to be happening, and when the danger is not one great temptation but a quiet drifting of the soul. Our hands follow our eyes. Our lives follow our focus. So the call of Hebrews is not merely, "Don't look at the danger." It's, "Look to Jesus."

"For the joy set before him." Joy was the goal, joy the motivation, joy the fuel. Jesus didn't endure the cross for the sake of pain. He didn't embrace shame because He enjoyed humiliation. He endured because of joy—joy in glorifying His Father, joy in redeeming His people, joy in accomplishing the mission of salvation. Joy was what lay on the other side of agony, and it was joy that made agony bearable.

Sarah can attest, along with every other woman who's ever given birth; there is a strange power in joy when pain has a purpose. Labor is not pretend pain by far. It's not mild discomfort. It's the kind of pain that takes over the whole body and demands all your attention. But there is a cry coming. There is a child coming. There is life on the other side of the agony. That doesn't reduce the pain but it does make the pain worth enduring.

That's only a faint shadow of what Hebrews is showing us. Jesus didn't endure nails, mockery, shame, forsakenness, and the wrath of Almighty God because suffering had some beauty of its own. He endured because joy was set before Him. The joy of pleasing His Father. The joy of redeeming His people. The joy of bringing sons and daughters into glory. The joy of taking sinners like you and me and making us family. Joy didn't make the cross lighter. Love did not make the nails softer. The agony was real. Every breath hurt. Every moment pressed down on Him with a weight we cannot comprehend. But love held Him there, and joy carried Him forward. For the glory of His Father and the salvation of His people, Jesus endured until redemption was finished.

"He endured the cross." To endure is to hold firm, to remain under a crushing weight without giving in. The cross was the most brutal instrument of death that Rome had to offer. Yet Jesus bore it because he knew what it would accomplish. The nails and the Roman guards were not the worst element of that torture. On that cross, Jesus took the full weight of the wrath of God that was intended for His chosen people. He exhausted that wrath and satisfied it completely. Theologically this is called "propitiation". It's the idea that Jesus completely satisfied or satiated the wrath of God for every sin that every child of God would have ever been guilty of.

Imagine for a moment that I slapped you in the face. Yes, you. I found your address through Amazon or Books-A-Million or wherever it is you bought this book. I pulled up in my Jeep, walked to your front door, and rang the doorbell. How epic would it be if someone rang your doorbell right now? If that happens to you, you have to let me know. Sorry, back to the analogy.

If I slapped you in the face, you might slap me back.
That might be the worst thing that happens to me.
Maybe you call the police and tell them some random
author showed up at your house and just slapped you.
Reasonable response, honestly.

Then the police officer arrives and confronts me.
Instead of calmly and rationally explaining myself, what
if I just reach out and slap him too? What happens to
me next? That's right: a taser, handcuffs, and a very
uncomfortable ride in the back of a squad car. I make it
downtown, stand before the judge, and ask to approach
the bench. Against everyone's better judgment, the
judge says yes, and I slap him too. What happens then?
"Book 'em, Danno."

Now let's say I somehow escape custody, continue my
cheek-slapping spree, make my way to the White
House, and slap the president of the United States of
America. That would likely be the end of life as I knew it.
At minimum, I am not making it home in time for dinner.

In each case, the action itself did not change. It was still
a slap. What changed was the dignity and authority of
the person offended. The greater the worth of the one
offended, the greater the offense. The greater the
offense, the greater the consequence. That helps us
understand why even what we call a "little sin" is not
little before God. Your little lie is not worthy of judgment
merely because of how much visible damage it caused
on earth. It's worthy of judgment because of the infinite
holiness, worth, and glory of the One you sinned
against.

Because God's worth is infinite, sin against Him carries an infinite seriousness. Every sin is not merely a broken rule. It's treason against the King of glory. It's the creature lifting his hand against the Creator. It's dust declaring war on the One who formed it. We don't feel the weight of that like we should, but heaven does. God does.

So when Jesus took the wrath of God for every sin His people had ever committed or ever would commit, He did not endure a small thing. He bore the full judgment owed to every trespass. The only way Christ could bear that wrath is if He Himself had infinite worth. And He does. He is God the Son. He is not merely a noble man suffering for a cause. He is the eternal Son standing in the place of His people, bearing what we could never survive, satisfying what we could never satisfy, and exhausting the wrath we could never escape.

Jesus endured what human language cannot fully name. Every word we reach for feels too small. Pain. Agony. Wrath. Judgment. Shame. None of them can carry the full weight of what happened at Calvary. He endured all of it in perfect obedience to His Father and in immeasurable love for His people.

But it was not only pain Christ endured. It was also shame and disgrace.

"Despising the shame." Crucifixion wasn't just torture. It was public humiliation. Jesus was stripped, mocked, jeered at by His enemies, and abandoned by His friends. He endured the kind of shame meant to break a man's spirit. But He "despised" it. That doesn't mean He pretended it was not real. It means He counted it as nothing compared to the joy set before Him. The shame was real, but it was not ultimate. The disgrace was brutal, but it was not final. Joy stood on the other side of the cross, and Jesus endured until the work was finished.

This is what Christ did. And it was fueled by unimaginable joy.

Sacrificial Joy

Jesus shows us the pattern. The cross was not endured by gritting His teeth and emptying Himself of all emotion. He endured the cross by the means of joy. Sacrifice and joy are not opposites in the Christian life. Sacrifice and joy are companions. The world says endurance comes by raw willpower, but Jesus shows us something different. True treasure-hunting is done with a joy-driven endurance.

Joy is not a shallow well but a deep ocean. Theologically, joy is the settled gladness rooted in God's character, secured by Christ's finished work, and applied to our hearts by the Holy Spirit. It's the fruit of knowing God and holding tightly to His promises. But joy is also deeply experiential. Joy can be tasted, felt; it can be known intimately. It warms the heart when all else grows cold. It lightens our burdens when they should crush us. It gives songs in the night and laughter even with tears are on our face.

This is why Nehemiah told Israel when they were broken by their sin and undone by conviction: "Do not grieve, for the joy of the Lord is your strength" (Neh. 8:10). Their repentance was real and their tears were justified. But God called them to embrace His joy, because joy is what would carry them forward in obedience.

So it is for us. Joy isn't optional in the Christian life, it's the strength that sustains us. Without joy, sacrifice becomes senseless. Without joy, obedience becomes impossible, and trials are unbearable. With joy, however, even the cross itself could be endured. If the Son of God walked His path fueled by joy, how much more must we?

All this talk of joy and it's just dawned on me, I've not defined it yet.

Webster's 1828 dictionary defines joy as "the passion or emotion excited by the acquisition or expectation of good." I like that. Joy isn't cold or mechanical. It's not the spiritual version of gritting your teeth and saying, "Everything's fine," when clearly everything is not fine. Joy is an affection. It's a real gladness of the heart, that sings and strengthens. Joy is felt deep in the soul.

Joy is stirred by "the acquisition or expectation of good." Joy shows up when some good is either possessed or promised. That means Christian joy is never floating around in the air by itself. It has an object. It is attached to something. Or better stated, it's attached to Someone. Our joy is rooted in Christ, who has been given to us and who has promised Himself to us forever.

Webster goes on to say, "Joy is a delight of the mind, from the consideration of the present or assured approaching possession of a good." That gives us another facet. Joy isn't mindless emotion. It comes from consideration. You think about what is true. You turn the promise over in your mind. You look at Christ. You look at the cross. You look at the empty tomb. You look at the throne. You look at the inheritance kept in heaven. And as the mind considers the good God has given and promised, the heart begins to rise.

So joy has many facets. Joy is satisfaction in God. It's the heart saying, "Christ is enough," even when everything around me says I need more. Joy is deeper than happiness. Happiness often depends on what's happening, but joy rests on what God has said. Joy is longing pointed in the right direction, the ache of the soul for the fullness of what Christ has promised. Joy is strength for suffering, because it tells the weary believer that pain is not final and loss is not ultimate. And joy is holy affection. It's feeling, but feeling trained by truth.

Joy is the fuel of treasure hunters. Joy is the strength that helps us keep digging, not because we love hardship, but because we know what lies ahead. We keep going because Christ is better. We keep digging because the treasure is real. We keep enduring because the joy set before us is not imaginary, fragile, or far-fetched. It is as certain as the risen Christ Himself.

What A Gift
Think of the last time you stumbled onto the perfect gift for someone you loved. Not the ordinary kind of gift, but the once-in-a-lifetime kind. The kind you knew was going to completely blow them away! Maybe you worked tirelessly to craft it. Maybe the idea dropped on you like a spark from heaven. Either way, you couldn't

wait to give it. The thought of their reaction kept you smiling for days or even weeks on end. You wrapped it, you guarded it, you anticipated the moment—not because you wanted to receive anything, but because the joy of giving was already spilling over before the gift was even opened.

And then came the moment. You gave it, and their face lit up. Maybe they gasped, "Where did you come up with this? How did you think of that?" Maybe they shook their head in disbelief at the time or effort it must have taken. Their joy was real. But in that moment, as sweet as it is to receive, the joy of giving ran deeper still. The receiver's joy couldn't touch the fullness of the giver's joy.

That is the crux of treasure hunting. We're not simply hunting for what we can keep. We're laboring, we're sacrificing, enduring, so that one day we'll stand before Jesus with eternal gifts in our hands. Every act of obedience, every step of faith, every sacrifice for His name is another gift wrapped in anticipation. And when that day comes, when the vault is opened and we lay those treasures at his feet, the joy of giving will overwhelm every earthly pleasure we've ever known.

This is how joy is the Christian's fuel. Sacrifice makes sense only in light of that future moment. The world looks at our endurance and thinks it's madness. But the joy set before us is worth everything.

If Mel Fisher could press on after storms, financial ruin, and even the death of his son—all for coins that could be stolen behind museum glass—what excuse do we have for our half-hearted pursuit of Christ? If an unrighteous man would endure that for earthly treasure, how much more should we endure for the eternal treasure of Jesus Himself? His obsession with gold indicts our apathy toward God.

So lift your eyes. Fix them on Christ. Run your race with joy as the fuel. Every gift you prepare now, every treasure you store in heaven, is fueling the greatest joy you will ever know. The joy of giving to the One who gave Himself for you.

Field Notes

This week, choose on "hard thing" you would normally avoid, and do it. Do it not out of duty, but for the joy set before you. Don't wait for the perfect moment. Let joy carry you into the difficult moment, and watch how it changes the way you endure.

- Share your faith even if the conversation feels awkward.
- Serve sacrificially even when you're exhausted.
- Rejoice openly in Christ even if others mock you.

And when you do, record it in your FIELD NOTES.

"Today I endured _______ because my eyes are on the joy of Christ."

Let that line become a testimony, not of your strength, but of the joy of Christ carrying you through.

A Final Word

Treasure hunters don't quit when the digging gets hard. They press on because the treasure is worth the sweat. It's worth the storms and the scars that might come. So it is with us. Jesus endured the cross because joy was stronger than sorrow. And that same joy is set before us. The Christian life is not grim duty; it's a glad pursuit. Fix your eyes on Jesus, look full into his wonderful face. And the things of this world will grow strangely dim, in the light of his glory and grace.

CHAPTER SIX

COUNTED AS TREASURE

Sometimes treasure doesn't look like treasure at all. For months, Mel Fisher's crew had been working stretches of seabed off Florida's coast that looked like nothing but endless sand. Dive after dive turned up little more than mud and shells. Many would have written it off as worthless ground.

Fisher, however, refused to quit. He and his team tinkered with a new invention they called "the mailbox." It was a system that diverted the boat's propellers downward, blasting away layers of sand to uncover whatever was hidden beneath. At first, it looked like another dead end. Just more water. More sand. More disappointment.

Then, one day, the mailbox cleared the sediment and revealed what no one expected—gold. Fisher's divers surfaced with 1,033 Spanish coins, glittering proof that riches were buried in what had looked like barren ground. What others dismissed as empty ocean floor had been hiding unimaginable wealth all along.

That's exactly what Jesus tells us about eternal treasure. It doesn't glimmer on the surface. Often it hides in the ordinary, the overlooked, especially in the places the world passes by as worthless. But for those who keep digging, what looks like nothing can turn out to be eternal gold.

1 Timothy 6:17-19
Paul's sentence builds like a staircase, each phrase stepping higher toward the vision of eternal treasure. "As for the rich in this present age, charge them not to be haughty, nor to set their hopes on the uncertainty of riches, but on God, who richly provides us with everything to enjoy. They are to do good, to be rich in good works, to be generous and ready to share, thus storing up treasure for themselves as a good foundation for the future, so that they may take hold of that which is truly life."

He begins with the simple call to "do good." Treasure, in Paul's mind, is not abstract. It's not ethereal or mystical. Treasure is lived faithfulness. Paul shows us that heavenly treasure takes shape in real obedience. It shows up in the daily choices of those who belong to Christ.

Then Paul says, "to be rich in good works." The contrast is shocking. Some long to be rich with gold, land, possessions, influence, or whatever else can be counted or admired. Paul says the real wealth of the believer is measured in good works. The riches that count are not what line your pockets, but what flows from your hands in service to Christ.

Now, we need to say this clearly. Good works are not the purchase price of eternal life. Paul is not teaching that we buy our way into heaven one kind deed at a time. Salvation is by grace alone, through faith alone, in Christ alone. But once Christ has saved us, obedience matters more than we often realize. The works themselves do not save us, but they are not throwaway moments either. They are not spiritual loose change. Every act of obedience to the Word is obedience to Jesus, and every act of obedience to Jesus is treasure being stored. That means the small moments are not small. The quiet yes to God. The temptation resisted. The forgiveness extended when every part of your flesh wants to keep the debt open. The generosity nobody sees. These are not meaningless acts floating away into the air. These are the gold and jewels of the kingdom. These are the treasures heaven keeps.

Paul goes on, "to be generous and ready to share." This is not a slog out of duty but an eagerness. Paul pictures a believer on the lookout, scanning for opportunities to give. Generosity is treasure because it mirrors the heart of God, who so loved the world that He gave. The generous Christian is not losing treasure. He is moving treasure into the only vault that cannot be broken.

Then Paul points us to the future: "thus storing up treasure for themselves as a good foundation for the future." Paul does not treat good works as sentimental gestures that vanish as soon as they are done. He says they are stored. That means obedience has a future. The believer's faithfulness is gathered up, remembered by God, and kept for the day when every hidden thing will be brought into the light. Unlike earthly wealth, these deposits are untouchable by moth, rust, and thieves. They form a foundation.

But heaven's treasure is not a reward we use to admire ourselves. The crowns of the saints will not be monuments to human achievement. They will be trophies of grace. One day, we will stand before Christ with nothing to brag about and nothing to boast in except Him. And yet, by His grace, the obedience He worked in us will not be wasted. Christ gives the command, Christ supplies the strength, Christ receives the obedience, and Christ preserves the reward. So when we finally lay those crowns before Him, we will not be showing Him what we did for Him. We will be giving back what His grace produced in us.

And finally, Paul gives us the goal: "so that they may take hold of that which is truly life." This is the climax. True life, eternal life, the life that cannot be purchased or stolen, is the treasure toward which all these works point. By God's grace, the believer's ordinary faithfulness is not a means of obtaining that life, but the evidence that it is truly theirs.

In just two verses, Paul reframes wealth, generosity, obedience, and even our understanding of eternal life itself. Treasure is not what we hoard. Treasure is what Christ produces through our obedience and keeps for the day we see Him face to face. What is stored up through simple faithfulness is kept safe in heaven's vault until the day every crown is laid at His feet.

Ordinary Days
When Paul speaks of treasure, he doesn't restrict it to martyrs or missionaries. He doesn't say, "Only those who preach to thousands" or "Only those who cross oceans for the gospel." He also doesn't restrict it to your local pastor. Instead, he calls every believer to do good, to be rich in good works, to be generous and ready to

share. Treasure isn't limited to the extraordinary, it's woven into the fabric of every ordinary day.

It's Wednesday right now as I'm writing this. Who else has to say, Wed-Nes-Day in their heads in order to spell it correctly? Just another ordinary Wednesday. I did it again. Except tomorrow is my twenty-first wedding anniversary. So at first glance, it might be just another day of the week, but for Sarah and me, it's a momentous week. As a married couple, we'll finally be able to drink legally. That joke might be lost on some of you, and I'm fine with that.

But that's how ordinary days work. They often look plain from the outside. Just another Wednesday. Just another morning. Just another commute. Just another dinner to cook, email to answer, child to correct, spouse to love, bill to pay, brother to encourage, temptation to resist, prayer to whisper, sin to confess, person to forgive. Nothing about it feels historic. Nobody's writing a biography about how faithfully you loaded the dishwasher or chose not to answer harshly when you really had a sentence locked and loaded.

But heaven sees with different eyes. What feels ordinary to us may be one of the places where obedience is being quietly stored as treasure. The day may not announce itself as important. It may not come with music, lighting, or a narrator saying, "This next decision will matter forever." It just comes as Wednesday. And yet Wednesday is filled with chances to treasure Christ. The small choices of faithfulness are not small because they happen on ordinary days. They're precious because they are offered to an extraordinary Savior.

I'm reminded here of something John Owen wrote in The Mortification of Sin. Owen warned that we cannot measure a believer's faithfulness merely by what the battle looks like from the outside. One man may seem calm and well-ordered simply because his natural temperament never had much taste for a particular sin. Another man may have to fight that same sin every day with tears, prayer, watchfulness, and trembling obedience. From the outside, the first man may look stronger. But heaven may know that the second man has fought harder, trusted Christ more desperately, and offered greater faithfulness in the struggle.

Heaven counts what the world overlooks. We can easily recognize certain "obvious" treasures. A sermon faithfully preached, a missionary sent to the nations, a church built where none existed before. These are real treasures, and rightly celebrated. But Scripture insists that the hidden works, the quiet obediences, are no less precious in the eyes of Jesus.

Every Christ-centered act of faithfulness counts. A cup of cold water given in His name (Matthew 10:42), a moment of endurance under trial (James 1:12), a word of encouragement offered in obscurity (1 Thessalonians 5:11). All of it is treasure, and not one of these deposits will be lost.

The world measures treasure in applause, or wealth, or fame. In our Christian culture today, we measure it often in church size or other meaningless benchmarks. But the kingdom of God weighs out your treasure in faithfulness. And faithfulness is found in the everyday.

Small Things

Scripture doesn't treat small faithfulness as small. That's where this whole idea comes from. I didn't invent the thought that an ordinary Wednesday can be filled with eternal treasure. The Bible keeps pressing this into us again and again. God sees what the world misses, and loves what the world ignores. He treasures faithfulness in places where nobody is paying attention.

Micah says it plainly: "He has told you, O man, what is good; and what does the LORD require of you but to do justice, and to love kindness, and to walk humbly with your God?" (Mic. 6:8). That sounds almost too ordinary, doesn't it? Do justice. Love kindness. Walk humbly. No fireworks. No platform. Just a life steadily moving with God in the right direction. But the Lord calls that good. A humble walk with God doesn't look impressive to the world. But this is the same world that applauds pure evil and wants to feed to your kids.

Jesus tells the same truth in the parable of the talents. The master says, *"Well done, good and faithful servant. You have been faithful over a little; I will set you over much. Enter into the joy of your master"* (Matt. 25:21) Faithful over a little. Don't rush past that. The Lord does not despise "a little." He honors it. He rewards it. The servant was not praised because he did something flashy enough to get everyone's attention. He was praised because he was faithful with what had been placed in his hands.

Paul presses it even further when he says, "So, whether you eat or drink, or whatever you do, do all to the glory of God" (1 Cor. 10:31). Eating and drinking are about as ordinary as it gets. Nobody puts "ate lunch to the glory of God" on a résumé. But Paul says even the most basic parts of life can be caught up into worship. The ordinary becomes holy when it's done unto the Lord.

Then he says it again in Colossians: "Whatever you do, work heartily, as for the Lord and not for men, knowing that from the Lord you will receive the inheritance as your reward. You are serving the Lord Christ" (Col. 3:23–24). Whatever you do. Not just preaching. Not just missions. Not just the things that feel obviously spiritual. Work. Labor. Service. The task in front of you. The thing you would rather not do. The job nobody notices. When it's done for Christ, it's not wasted. You're serving the Lord.

So yes, heaven counts Wednesdays. Heaven counts your quiet obedience. Heaven counts the unseen faithfulness. Heaven counts the work done with a Godward heart. The Bible doesn't let us divide life into meaningful spiritual moments and meaningless ordinary ones. In Christ, the ordinary is never merely ordinary. Every small act of faithfulness offered to Him is seen, received, and kept by the Lord who misses nothing.

Edward Kimball

History remembers the name D. L. Moody, one of the most influential evangelists of the nineteenth century. Moody was not merely a preacher with a large platform. He became a force in American evangelical life. After moving to Chicago, he poured himself into evangelistic work, started a Sunday school for poor children, helped establish a church, worked with the YMCA, preached to enormous crowds in America and Britain, and became tied to institutions that still shape Christian ministry today. Chicago still bears the marks of his labor. Moody Bible Institute, Moody Church, Moody Publishers: his name did not vanish quietly into the footnotes. It stayed.

But almost no one remembers the man who first told him about Christ.

Edward Kimball wasn't a preacher or a missionary. Edward Kimball was a Sunday school teacher. Just a faithful, ordinary, unnoticed Sunday school teacher. When he learned that one of the boys in his class, a teenager working in a shoe shop, didn't understand the gospel, he made it his quiet mission to visit him. Kimball walked nervously into that store, found Moody among the shoes, and spoke to him about Christ. Moody later traced the beginning of his Christian life to that conversation.

Think about that. Kimball did not walk into the shoe store that day thinking, "Well, I suppose I'll go change the course of evangelical history before lunch." He walked in nervous. He walked in ordinary. He walked in with one boy on his mind. No crowds. No pulpit. No choir softly singing in the background. Just a Sunday school teacher, a young shoe salesman, and the gospel.

From there, the ripple widened. Through Moody's life and ministry, thousands upon thousands heard the gospel. Moody's influence touched men like F. B. Meyer, whose preaching shaped J. Wilbur Chapman, whose ministry overlapped with and encouraged the evangelistic world that produced Billy Sunday. Sunday's preaching, in turn, helped stir the kind of revivalism that marked the ministry of Mordecai Ham, the evangelist who preached the night Billy Graham was saved. The ripple is undeniable. One nervous Sunday school teacher walked into a shoe shop to talk to one teenage boy about Jesus, and generations later, the waves are still crashing.

On earth, Kimball's life looked small. He never founded a mission like Moody did. He never filled a stadium like Graham did. But heaven recorded his faithfulness. What to you and me would undoubtedly seem insignificant was, in reality, eternal treasure.

Kimball's story is proof that treasure is found in everyday life lived boldly for Jesus. A quiet conversation. A hesitant act of obedience. A small step of faith. These are not worthless in the light of heaven. God sees each one. Jesus uses each one. The Father values each one. And they are all counted as gold.

Field Notes
This time, don't add something new to your life. Instead, take something ordinary you're already doing and deliberately treasure it as eternal.

 - See the unseen.
 - Count as gold.

Write it down in your FIELD NOTES:

"Today I counted ___ as treasure because Christ is worth it."

A Final Word
The world keeps score with numbers, applause, and fame. Heaven keeps score with faithfulness. Treasure-hunting is not about being impressive; it is about being faithful. Every hidden act of obedience is noticed, and remembered by God Himself.

One day, when all is revealed, you'll see how even the smallest deeds have been stored away as eternal treasure. They'll be all polished up real nice, and shining in the presence of Christ Himself. That's what awaits the faithful. So, live for what lasts.

CHAPTER SEVEN

TREASURE FOUND

For sixteen years, Mel Fisher began every morning with the same stubborn words: "Today's the day."

It became more than a phrase. It was his rallying cry. His daily defiance against disappointment. His way of standing on the edge of another long day, looking out over the same stretch of ocean that had refused him yesterday, and saying, "Maybe today the sea gives it back."

For sixteen years, he said it to weary crews before they set out to comb the ocean floor again. Dive after dive turned up mud, broken pieces, scattered clues, and just enough hope to keep them from quitting. Storms battered their boats. Lawsuits drained their resources. Grief struck their family. The ocean did not surrender the treasure quickly or kindly. Still, every sunrise, Mel said it again.

"Today's the day."

Most days, it wasn't.

That is the painful part of any real treasure hunt. The motto sounds heroic in hindsight, but in the middle of the hunt, it must have felt almost ridiculous. How many times can a man say, "Today's the day," only to climb back onto the boat empty-handed? How many times can hope rise with the sun and sink again before evening? How many times can you tell yourself the treasure is real when all you can see is sand?

Then came July 20, 1985.

Mel's son Kane was working the waters when the mailbox system churned away layers of sand from the ocean floor. And there it was. Not another hint. Not another almost. Not another little piece to keep the dream alive for one more week. Treasure.

Silver bars stacked like bricks. Coins glittering in the sunlight. Jewels scattered across the seafloor. The lost wealth of the Atocha had finally come out of hiding. After sixteen years of searching, the hunt was over. Kane radioed the words his father had waited so long to hear: "Put away the charts. We've got the mother lode."

Put away the charts. That line gets me. For years, the charts mattered. The maps mattered. The theories mattered. The coordinates mattered. The search patterns, the dives, the equipment, the guesses, the next place to look. But once the treasure was found, the charts had served their purpose. You don't keep studying the map when you're standing on the X. You don't keep asking where the treasure is when it's lying in front of you. The thing hoped for had become the thing held.

The celebration that followed was electric. Fisher's daily mantra had been vindicated. "Today's the day" was no longer stubborn hope. It was history. The treasure he had hunted for had surfaced at last. No more speculation. No more desperation. No more wondering whether the years had been wasted. The treasure was real.

One of the emeralds found, a rather large one I might add, was later cut into the famed Atocha Star and given by Mel to his wife, Dolores. It wasn't merely hoarded or locked away as another object in a collection. It became a gift. A treasure found became a treasure given.

That's how treasure hunts end. Not with permanent longing. Not with charts forever spread across the table. They end with discovery. They end with joy. They end with the hunter holding what he had always believed was there.

One day, our own hunt will end the same way. Faith will become sight. Hope will become history. And the map will give way to the face of Jesus. The prayers, the obedience, the sacrifices, the quiet faithfulness, the years of saying, "Today's the day," while still waiting for the fullness of the promise, all of it will find its answer in Him.

And when that Day comes, we will not surface from the depths with rusting coins or jewels that can be stolen. We will stand before the King with treasures eternal, ready to lay them down in worship before the One who was the treasure all along.

2 Corinthians 5:10
Paul writes in 2 Corinthians 5:10, "For we must all appear before the judgment seat of Christ, so that each

one may receive what is due for what he has done in the body, whether good or evil."

Every believer will stand before Christ. Let that sentence sit for a moment. Not a general Idea. Not a vague future. Not "humanity" in some abstract sense. You. Me. Every believer who has ever named the name of Jesus will stand before Him. The One we have sung to, prayed to, preached about, trusted, failed, followed, ignored, loved, and longed for. We will stand before Christ.

The word Paul uses for "appear" carries the idea of being made visible, laid bare, or revealed. Nothing will be hidden. No act forgotten. No motive overlooked. No secret faithfulness lost in the cracks of history. And no small obedience dismissed because no one on earth noticed it. Everything will be brought into the light.

Now that might sound terrifying at first, but for the believer it should not be heard as a threat of condemnation. This isn't Christ reopening the case against you. That's how I understood it years ago. I thought that when we stand before the Lord on that day, we'll have a big projector screen slowly roll down and all our failures will be on display for the rest of my brothers and sisters to see. No. The court case was closed and the evidence dealt with on the cross. "There is therefore now no condemnation for those who are in Christ Jesus."(Rom. 8:1) The judgment seat of Christ is not the place where Jesus decides whether His blood was enough. It was enough. It is enough. It will always be enough.

Paul gives us that picture in 1 Corinthians 3:12–15. Some works are like gold, silver, and precious stones. They endure the fire. Others are like wood, hay, and straw. They may have looked impressive for a while, but when the fire tests them, nothing lasting remains.

This is the judgment seat of Christ, the bēma. It's a place of evaluation, not damnation. A place where works are revealed, weighed, and rewarded. What was done in faith and love for Christ remains. What was done in selfishness, pride, unbelief, or sin is burned away. Pause there for a second. They will be burned away. Yes, I'm sure many of the things I've done "for Jesus" will be burned away in that moment. But when you think about it, that is actually deeply comforting. Even the record of those failures will be cleared away. Jesus will take all that wood, hay, and stubble and set fire to it, so I don't have to stare at those failures for all eternity. All that will remain are the things that make much of Christ. All that will remain is the good. And when you're like me, and you've done a whole lot of stupid . . . well, let's just say I ain't mad at that purifying fire.

And on that Day, the only thing that will matter is whether our lives were lived by faith, in love, and for Christ. That is not meant to make us frantic. It is meant to make us focused. If Christ will one day reveal what was treasure and what was straw, then wisdom says we should start asking now what will survive the fire. Not because we are trying to earn His love, but because we already have it. Not because we are terrified He will cast us away, but because we want to bring Him what remains.

This is why Revelation 4 matters so much. Second Corinthians 5 shows us the day our works are revealed. Revelation 4 shows us what the rewards are for. The treasure that survives the fire is not finally for our display. It is for His glory.

Revelation 4:10-11
The apostle John gives us the heavenly picture in Revelation 4:10–11: "...they cast their crowns before the throne, saying, 'Worthy are you, our Lord and God, to receive glory and honor and power, for you created all things, and by your will they existed and were created.'"

John sees the elders before the throne of God, and they have crowns. Scripture never treats heavenly reward as imaginary or unspiritual. The Lord really does remember what is done for Him. He really does speak of treasure, reward, crowns, and inheritance. We may feel nervous talking this way, as if reward language somehow competes with grace, but the Bible has no such embarrassment. Grace doesn't void the concept of reward. Grace makes reward possible.

But notice what happens next. The elders receive crowns, but they do not keep them as trophies. Almost as soon as the reward is seen in their hands, it's placed back before the throne. That tells us what heavenly treasure is for. It's not the end of worship, as though God rewards us and then we wander off to admire what we've received. The reward becomes part of the worship. The crown becomes an offering. What Christ gives to His people is returned to Him in praise, because the treasure was never meant to stop with the redeemed. It was always meant to magnify the Redeemer.

This is where heavenly reward becomes so beautiful. On earth, rewards often tempt us toward pride. Give a man a trophy, and he wants a shelf. Give him applause, and he wants a bigger room. I know this because I have a heart and, unfortunately, it came standard with pride. But heaven's not like that. In heaven, reward won't inflate our egos. These rewards are designed to ignite our worship.

The elders cast their crowns because they know where the crowns came from. "Worthy are you, our Lord and God, to receive glory and honor and power." Why? "For you created all things, and by your will they existed and were created." Everything begins with God. Everything exists by God. Everything is sustained by God. Every breath, every gift, every act of faithfulness, every ounce of strength, every moment of endurance, every crown earned by grace and received in glory, all of it traces back to Him.

These crowns then aren't monuments to human achievement. These crowns are testimonies of divine grace. If we receive any reward, it will be because Christ saved us, kept us, and Christ strengthened us. The crown may be placed in our hands, but it won't stay there long. The only natural response will be to lay it back down before Him.

And this is the part that makes the whole treasure-hunting life make sense. The treasure we store up is not finally for us to possess as though heaven were an eternal awards banquet with nameplates and applause. The treasure is for worship. The joy is not merely that we receive crowns. The joy is that we will have something to give back to Jesus. We'll have something real to lay before the One who gave Himself for us.

Think about that. After all the grace He's given, after all the mercy He's shown, after all the patience and forgiveness He's poured out, after all the times He held us fast when we would have wandered away, He will still give His people the joy of bringing Him treasure. Not because He needs it. Not because His glory is lacking. Not because the King of heaven is short on crowns. But because love delights to give. He delights to give us eternal life, and He also delights to give us the joy of giving back to Him.

Doesn't that just blow you away? Jesus knows the blessing of giving. He knows the joy of pouring out love. And in His kindness, He brings His people into that joy. From before the foundation of the world, He planned not only to save us, but to make our lives fruitful, reward what His grace produced, and then give us the joy of returning it all to Him in worship.

The twenty-four elders are the ones John sees casting their crowns before the throne, we should be honest about that. John doesn't stop to explain every detail of how their crowns relate to every believer's reward. But the scene shows us the pattern of heaven. The highest use of any crown is worship. The greatest joy of reward is not keeping it, admiring it, or comparing it. The greatest joy of reward is giving it back to the One who is worthy.

If we harmonize these two texts, the picture becomes clearer. Second Corinthians 5 tells us that treasure is real and will be tested. Revelation 4 shows us the purpose of treasure. It's not to display our worth, but to magnify His. The true joy of treasure hunting will not be found in clutching rewards to our chest, but in seeing every reward become an offering before the throne.

That's how the hunt ends. Not with treasure locked away in our own heavenly vault. Not with crowns stacked up so we can admire our spiritual résumé. The hunt ends with worship. It ends with every reward swallowed up in praise. It ends with the redeemed people of God joining heaven's song: "Worthy are you, our Lord and God."

The Treasure Was Always Christ
The treasure was never mainly crowns, rewards, mansions, or gold in heaven's vault. The treasure is Christ. Every reward is precious because it comes from Him. Every crown is precious because it can be laid before Him. Every act of obedience matters because it draws us nearer to Him and will one day be received by Him. Heaven's not glorious because the streets are gold. Heaven is glorious because Jesus is there.

That's been the point of the hunt all along. If you have Christ, you have treasure. If you lose everything and still have Him, you're rich. If you gain everything and don't have Him, you have nothing. "For what will it profit a man if he gains the whole world and forfeits his soul? Or what shall a man give in return for his soul?" (Matt 16:26) The true treasure hunter learns to say, "Give me Christ." Not, Christ as a means to better stuff. Not, Christ as a ticket to a nicer eternity. Christ Himself. The pearl of great price. The treasure hidden in the field. The One worth selling everything to have.

And every step of the hunt was grace. We don't come to that Day as self-made treasure hunters with impressive spiritual résumés in our hands. We come as sinners saved by grace, carried, corrected, strengthened by grace, and made fruitful by grace. Every faithful step was the grace of Christ in us, the hope of glory. Every act of obedience that survives the fire was grace. And every crown placed in our hands will be by His marvelous, infinite, matchless, grace.

That's what makes the reward so wonderful. Christ gives the command, Christ supplies the strength, Christ receives the obedience, Christ preserves the treasure, and then Christ gives us the joy of laying it all back at His feet. We will not stand before Him bragging about how well we hunted. We'll fall before Him amazed that He let us hunt at all.

If You Have Not Found Him
Before this book closes, I need to say one more thing. Maybe as you've read these pages, something has become painfully clear. You've loved the idea of heaven, but not Christ. You've wanted forgiveness, but not the King. Maybe you've wanted peace, comfort, family, success, or escape from judgment, but you have not wanted Jesus Himself. If that's true, then don't cover it up. Don't decorate it with religious language.

The call of Christ is not, "Admire Me from a distance." And it's not, "Use Me to get the life you wanted." It's not even, "Add Me to the treasures you already have." The call of Christ is, "Follow Me." Repentance means turning from sin, yes, but sin is never only the bad things we do. Sin is also the lesser treasures we love more than God.

To repent is to turn from the empty vaults of this world and come to Christ as the treasure your soul was made to find.

I have incredible news for you. I hope you're still here with me. The news is, Jesus receives sinners. He doesn't receive cleaned-up treasure hunters who already know how to dig in the right places. He receives the lost. He receives the guilty. He receives the proud, the greedy, the religious hypocrite, the exhausted pretender, and the person who just realized they've been holding fool's gold their entire life. Come to Him. Confess your sin. Stop trusting yourself. Stop trusting your goodness. Stop trusting your church attendance, your family name, your religious background, or your ability to do better next time. Trust Christ!

He lived the righteous life you have not lived. He died the death your sin deserves. He bore the wrath of God in the place of His people. He rose from the dead, and He now calls sinners to Himself. If you see Him today, not merely as useful, not merely as helpful, but as beautiful, worthy, and better than all else, then come. Lay down your sin. Lay down your excuses. Lay down your lesser treasures. Take hold of Christ by faith.

Because the treasure is not hidden from you now. He has been held out before you. Jesus Christ is the treasure. Repent and believe in Him.

And for those who belong to Him, today is still the day.
Today's the day to obey.
Today's the day to forgive.
Today's the day to give.

Today's the day to endure.
Today's the day to dig.

One day, the hunt will be over. Faith will become sight. The crowns will be cast. The treasure will be found. And we will see that Christ was worth it all.

Field Notes

This time, don't just make a swap for a day, or pick a single act for a week. Pause and name one area of your life where you will begin treasure hunting with eternity in view.

- Parenting.
- Work.
- Prayer.
- Generosity.
- Service.

Wherever it is, see it not as routine, but as preparation for the moment you will stand before Christ.

Write it down in your FIELD NOTES as a conscious gift you're preparing:

"I am beginning to store treasure in ______________, so that one day I may lay it at the feet of Jesus."

Conclusion
Life is the greatest treasure hunt ever offered—not with shovels in dirt or ships at sea, but with faith and obedience in Christ. The world chases riches to hoard; let them. We chase treasures to give. And when the hunt is over, the adventure doesn't end with vaults of gold for ourselves, but with joy overflowing as we cast every crown, every jewel, every act of faithfulness at the feet of Jesus.

Don't waste your hunt. Don't trade your days for rusting coins or fading applause. Live with eternity in view. Store up treasure where moth and rust cannot touch it. And prepare for the moment when you will stand before the King, with joy beyond imagining, and give Him all that your life has stored.

The hunt is on. The treasure is Christ. And the joy of giving it all back to Him will last forever.

www.ingramcontent.com/pod-product-compliance
Lightning Source LLC
Chambersburg PA
CBHW031445150726

47990CB00007B/2622